Relocation in Later Years

Relocation in Later Years

✦

Aging-in-Place in America's Urban Neighborhoods

Michael A. Fornaro, PhD

iUniverse, Inc.
New York Lincoln Shanghai

Relocation in Later Years
Aging-in-Place in America's Urban Neighborhoods

iUniverse books may be ordered through booksellers or by contacting:

iUniverse
2021 Pine Lake Road, Suite 100
Lincoln, NE 68512
www.iuniverse.com
1-800-Authors (1-800-288-4677)

ISBN-13: 978-0-595-36476-3 (pbk)
ISBN-13: 978-0-595-80908-0 (ebk)
ISBN-10: 0-595-36476-4 (pbk)
ISBN-10: 0-595-80908-1 (ebk)

Printed in the United States of America

This book is dedicated to my family and friends.
You have inspired me and continue to encourage me.
For your endless support and love I am truly grateful.

Contents

Foreword

American society will soon be overwhelmed with the number of older adults over the age of sixty-five. The question is where will they live? The answer is that many will live in neighborhoods in all of America's urban cities either by choice or by default. Our American society has a long history of assisting older people in the form of Social Security, meals for shut-ins, and medical insurance. However, Americans have fallen short in one arena that has a profound impact on the quality of day-to-day living - housing.

Housing that is well designed, suitably located, and affordable contributes to the ability of an older person to maintain his or her independence and to age in place. The current housing options available in urban neighborhoods are limited and are becoming a crucial factor in determining the physical, social, and emotional well-being of older adults.

Relocation in Later Years: Aging-in-Place in America's Urban Neighborhoods is an overview and discussion of the reasons older adults are forced into relocating. The decision to relocate is often a result of housing preferences among older adults living in urban neighborhoods and their degree of neighborhood satisfaction. I have developed strategies to both retain and attract older adults to urban neighborhoods and provided a foundation to advocate for (1) the development of elderly-friendly neighborhoods, and (2) middle-income and low-income older adults living in urban neighborhoods to have access to the same type of retirement amenities and benefits offered to the Multiple-Choice Generation with the development of the "Urban Continuum."

A research study conducted in June 2004 in Cleveland, Ohio, notes that current housing situations do not encourage older adults to remain in their homes, for example, limited housing options and choices in urban neighborhoods. For many of the residents who participated in the Return to City Movement research study, conducted in the Saint Hyacinth neighborhood in Cleveland, housing options and choices were limited to an institutional nursing home setting. Aging in place is not an option. As the cost of medical insurance and housing increases, many senior Americans will find themselves in a similar situation as they grow older.

Aging-in-place is the fastest-growing trend and direction in senior housing and in caring for our aging population. The trend is an outcome of the continuing increase in medical costs for older adults. Research studies have indicated that if older adults can remain in their existing homes longer and age in place, there would be less strain on federal health-care costs for older adults. Keeping older adults out of the medical system and out of a nursing home or institutional setting is a win-win situation for all.

The popularity of the continuing-care retirement community concept and the desire to let people grow old in their own homes and communities will make the "Urban Continuum" the next logical step in developing low- and middle-income senior housing in urban neighborhoods.

1

Housing America's Seniors

L eadership is needed to support planning processes and implementation efforts that improve the interface between the aging experience and the built environment. Public policy for both affordable and public housing is a necessary component of the action agenda that must be put into place if older adults are to be full participants in - and not cut off from - our society in the coming decades. The future direction of the housing industry for older adults will be to develop strategies that promote and encourage older residents to age in place. The following chapter will support this statement with statistical data that frames the current housing situation among older adults, the predicted needs for senior housing, and future housing alternatives for older adults.

In order to fully understand the housing demands the United States will face over the next 30 years, it is important to understand the manner in which our population is aging. The data provided in the following section was compiled primarily from Internet releases from the United States Bureau of the Census and the National Center for Health Statistics.

The U.S. older population, referring to persons aged sixty-five and older, numbered 35 million in 2000 according to the latest year for which data is available. This age cohort represents more than 12% of the United States population, about 1 in every 8 Americans. The number of older Americans increased by almost 4 million or 12% since 1990, compared to an increase of just more than 13% for the under-sixty-five population. However, the number of Americans aged forty-five to sixty-five - the baby boomers who will reach sixty-five over the next 2 decades - increased by 34% during this period.

For the sake of this discussion, baby boomers are defined as all noninstitutionalized older adults over the age of fifty-five. The "Multiple-Choice" generation refers only to older adults in the income bracket of $75,000 a year or higher. This group can claim only 5.5% of the entire fifty-five-plus population - fewer than 3 million of the over 53 million older adults have multiple housing options.

According to the U.S. census data, 58% of the entire fifty-five and over population has an annual income of less than $20,000 per year. The senior housing market continues to build large-scale continuing-care retirement communities with entry fees that start at $200,000 and cap out at $450,000. This high-end lifestyle does not meet the housing needs of the majority of our aging population. Many older adults who have bought into the continuing-care retirement community lifestyle have found the increases in monthly rents and fees for services make it too expensive to stay.

According to the U.S. census in 2000, there were over 20 million older women and over 14 million older men, or a sex ratio of 143 women for every 100 men. The female-to-male sex ratio increases with age, ranging from 117 for the age group between sixty-five and sixty-nine to a high of 245 for persons eighty-five years of age and over.

Since 1900, the percentage of Americans over the age of sixty-five has more than tripled. This portion of the population has increased 11 times from over 3 million older adults to 35 million older adults. The older population itself is getting even older. In the year 2000, older adults between the ages of sixty-five and seventy-four accounted for over 18 million older adults. This group was 8 times larger than in 1900. The age group between seventy-five and eighty-four accounted for over 12 million adults and was 16 times larger than in 1900. The age group of eighty-five and older, which accounted for slightly over 4 million older adults, is reported to be 34 times larger than in 1900.

In the year 2000, persons reaching the age of sixty-five had an average life expectancy of an additional 17 years. Women had a life expectancy of 19 more years; men, 16 more years. Therefore, a child born in the year 2000 could expect to live to be over seventy-nine years old, which is about

30 years longer than the life expectancy of a child born in 1900. Much of this increase occurred because of reduced death rates for children and young adults. However, the past two decades have also seen reduced death rates for the population between the ages of sixty-five and eighty-four, especially for men, by 19%. Life expectancy at age sixty-five increased by only two years between 1900 and 1960 but has increased by more than 3 years since 1960.

In the year 2000, over 2 million older adults celebrated their sixty-fifth birthday. That is slightly over 5,000 per day. In the same year, about 2 million older adults aged sixty-five or older died, resulting in an annual net increase of approximately 238,000, or 650 per day.

According to the 2000 U.S. census, there were just over 50,000 older adults over the age of one hundred. This age cohort increased 35% from the year 1990.

The "graying" American population can also be defined by the following characteristics: ethnicity, educational level, marital status, and living arrangements.

Ethnicity - The U.S. Census Bureau in 2000 purported that 16% of adults over the age of sixty-five were minorities. The largest minority percentage of 8% represented African-Americans. Asian or Pacific Islanders represented less than 3%, and American Indians or Native Alaskans represented less than 1%. Older adults of Hispanic origin, who may be of any race, represented over 5% of the older population. In addition, less than 1% of older adults age sixty-five and over identified themselves as being of two or more races.

Educational Level - According to data collected by the U.S. Census Bureau in 2000, the educational level of the older population is increasing. Between 1970 and 2001, the percentage of older adults who completed high school rose from 28% to 70%. About 17% of older adults had a bachelor's degree in 2004.

The percentage of older adults who completed high school varied considerably by race and ethnic origin: 74% of whites, 63% of Asians and Pacific Islanders, 51% of African-Americans, and 35% of Hispanics.

Marital Status - Older men were much more likely to be married than were older women, according to the 2000 U.S. Census Bureau. For example, 73% of men were married and only 41% of women were married. Almost half of all older women in 2001 were widows. There were over 4 times as many widows, about 9 million, compared to only 2 million widowers.

Divorced and separated, including married-spouse absent, older adults represented only 10% of all older adults in 2001. However, this percentage has increased significantly since 1990, when approximately 7% of the older adult population was divorced or separated.

Living Arrangements - Data from the U.S. Census Bureau in 2000 showed that over 55% of older noninstitutionalized adults lived with their spouse. Approximately 10 million or 73% of older men, and over 7 million or 41% of older women, lived with their spouse. The number of older adults living with their spouse decreased with age, especially for women. Only 28% of women age seventy-five and older lived with a spouse.

In 2000, 30% (slightly over 9 million) of all noninstitutionalized older adults lived alone. The 9 million older adults comprise 7 million men (or 40% of men) and 2 million women (17% of women). The number of older adults living alone increases with advanced age. Among women age seventy-five and older, for example, 50% lived alone.

In 1997, grandparents aged sixty-five and over accounted for 600,000 older adults who maintained households in which grandchildren were present. In addition, 500,000 grandparents over the age of sixty-five lived in parent-maintained households in which their grandchildren were present.

While a relatively small number of older adults - 1 million older adults, or 4% of older adults over the age of sixty-five - lived in nursing homes in 2000, the percentage increases dramatically with age, ranging from 1% for adults between the ages of sixty-five and seventy-four to almost 5% for older adults between the ages of seventy-five and eighty-four and 18% for older adults over the age of eighty-four.

Future projections indicate that the Multiple-Choice Generation will continue to grow significantly in the future. This growth slowed somewhat during the 1990s because of the relatively small number of babies born during the Great Depression of the 1930s. But the older population will burgeon between 2010 and 2030 when the baby boom generation reaches age sixty-five.

By 2030, about 70 million older adults will be part of the Multiple-Choice Generation, more than twice their number in 2000. Older adults over the age of sixty-five represented 12% of the population in 2000 but are expected to grow to be 20% of the population by 2030.

In the future, minority populations are projected to represent 25% of the older adult population in 2030, up from 16% in 2000. Between 1999 and 2030, the white population over the age of sixty-five is projected to increase by 81% compared with an increase of 200% for older adult minorities. Hispanics over the age of sixty-five will increase by over 300%; African-Americans over the age of sixty-five will increase by over 113%; American Indians, Eskimos, and Aleuts over the age of sixty-five will increase by 147%; and Asians and Pacific Islanders over the age of sixty-five will increase by 285%.

Housing the Multiple-Choice Generation - According to the 2001 American Housing Survey (AHS), of the nearly 2 million households headed by older adults, 80% were owners and 20% were renters. In 2001 the median family income of older homeowners was $23,409. The median family income of older renters was $12,233. According to the survey, 41% of older adult householders spent more than one-fourth of their income on housing costs, compared to 39% for homeowners of all ages.

For homes occupied by older householders in 2001, the median year of construction was 1963 and 5% of the homes had physical problems.

When the survey was completed in 2001, the median value of homes owned by older persons was $107,398, compared to a median home value of $123,887 for all homeowners. About 73% of older homeowners in 2001 owned their homes free and clear.

The current state of housing available to the Multiple-Choice Generation, living in noninstitutional settings, can be divided into 2 broad categories: homeownership and rentals.

Homeownership - According to the 1995 AHS, over 20 million housing units were headed by an adult aged sixty-five or older. In that same year, there were approximately 97 million households. Of the more than 20 million households, 78%, or approximately 16 million older adults, owned their homes. According to past data, this percentage has increased from 74% reported in 1980. The American Housing Survey predicts that the percentage of homeownership by older adults will continue to increase over the next decade. This prediction is rooted in the current incidence of mortgage debt among older homeowners, which is very low. In fact, approximately 80% of older homeowners own their homes free and clear. According to the AHS, currently most older-owner households occupied single-family homes. Over 13 million older-owner households occupied single-family detached homes, and an additional 8% of older-owner households lived in manufactured homes; most of these homes had a median worth over $82,000. Over one-third, or 36% of older owners were single, and approximately 80% of older single-person owners were female.

Older adult renters, according to the American Housing Survey in 1995, comprised approximately 4 million older households. The likelihood of renting increased with age and was higher for minority households. In addition, renter households constituted a higher percentage of households headed by an individual aged seventy-five and older, about 25% in comparison to households headed by an individual between the ages of sixty-four and seventy-five, which was reported as just under 20%. In summary, renter households headed by an individual aged seventy-five or older accounted for approximately 53% of all older renter households.

The 2001 American Housing Survey indicates that older renters live in diverse types of structures and housing options such as apartment buildings, single-family detached homes, multifamily homes, manufactured homes, and condominiums.

Minority households were represented in the study as follows: African-American and Hispanic households represented 9% and 4%, respectively, of all older households, but 14% and 8% of older renter households. Thirty-four percent of older African-American households and 41% of older Hispanic households were renter households, compared with less than 20% of older white households.

Within the category of renters, single-person households constituted about 71% of all older renter households. Single female renters comprised the largest group of older renter households in 1995.

Housing Costs in 2004 - Approximately two-thirds, or 64%, of older households incurred monthly housing costs that were less than 30% of their current monthly income. However, about half of all older African-American households and half of all older Hispanic households spent 30% or more of their monthly income on housing costs.

Current research from the American Association of Retired People indicates that older renter households tended to face higher housing costs and have lower incomes with which to pay those costs than older-owner households. For example, older owners had median monthly housing costs of $282, compared to median monthly housing costs of $412 for older renters. About 48% of older renter households had annual family incomes of less than $10,000, compared with only 20% of older owners.

Once an individual starts to reach the latter stages of his or her life, it should be apparent that things are not quite what they used to be. This is not to say that there are many untrue generalizations made about the effects of aging on the elderly (individual), but statistically the elderly as a whole lack the ability to function as efficiently as they did in their younger years. It is important for them to realize that as they age they may have to reconsider their housing choices. These choices may include house sharing, restricted communities, age-restricted communities, congregate housing communities, and nonmedical residential care facilities.

There are several housing types that have been developed over the years to accommodate seniors. The problem is that many of these options do not exist where the majority of older adults will live in the future - urban neighborhoods. That is why it is essential for older adults to begin the planning for later-life housing needs before retirement, preferably when they are in their fifties. When planning for later-life housing, the elderly person needs to take into account the appropriateness associated with a house: a house designed to serve a sixty-five-year-old person likely won't be appropriate for a ninety-year-old person. Therefore, they will have to answer the question of whether they are willing to relocate some years after they have entered the latter years of their lives. For most people, the answer is yes. For others who choose not to relocate in their later years, the option to age in place should be available to them.

Another important factor to consider in planning for housing for the elderly is the elderly individual's financial circumstances. Most of the elderly at the retirement level are at their financial peaks, so it is important to realize that while their capital will remain stable upon retirement, it is probable that their consumable income will deteriorate. For that reason, the type of housing planned for in an individual's midfifties may have to be rethought. With this in mind, it would be beneficial for the elderly to have more than one housing option in mind during the planning process.

Today, there are several housing options and alternatives available to older adults. These choices include house sharing, restricted communities, age-restricted communities, congregate housing communities, and non-medical residential care facilities. The following is a brief analysis of the current housing options available.

Home sharing is an option in which family considerations play a big role in where the elderly are willing to live. One of the biggest fears that elderly people deal with is growing old alone in a place that they particularly do not care for. Moreover, most elderly would prefer to stay right where they are, preferably in their own homes. For these individuals, a perfect solution is shared housing. A shared-housing option is attractive to the elderly because it can involve living with other family members. The option of living with family members can be both beneficial and detrimental to the parties involved - warm companionship or never-ending disputes between the elderly and their relatives. That is why it is important for the parties to discuss how the situation might evolve as the homeowner ages.

Another aspect that may concern the parties to house sharing is the termination of the arrangement. Realistically, relationships often turn bitter with the passage of time; therefore, it is important for the homeowner to possess the right to terminate unilaterally. Of course, this agreement would have to require some period of notice - 2 weeks to a month is usually acceptable. The issue of notice is additionally important to protect the elderly homeowner if he or she is suffering from some illness at the time of the sudden departure.

Another issue to be addressed in a shared-housing situation is the issue of eviction for cause. The parties would probably have to agree that the homeowner can evict the housemate for cause, including acts of dishonesty, misuse of property, and other acts of moral turpitude, with only a 24-hour notice.

Shared housing is also very attractive financially. This attractiveness stems from the fact that the housemate will usually be paying rent to reside in the house with the elderly homeowner.

The Multiple-Choice Generation has more housing and community choices than the previous generation. Despite the attractiveness of living in one's own home, there are many older adults who may prefer the option to relocate. When pursuing the option to relocate, there are many options. The first option described in this section is planned communities. There is really no fixed definition of a "planned unit development." Most of these developments encompass (1) cluster or zero-lot line housing (without yards), (2) fee-simple detached or attached housing, (3) combined high-rise and low-rise units, or (4) mixed-use developments with a variety of elements. (The above elements vary to meet the dynamic needs of the elderly.)

If this housing option is exercised by the older individual, it is important for him or her to know that he or she could be an owner in common of the planned unit development. This could be very attractive to a potential resident, since the majority of these facilities include common ownership of recreational facilities, such as a swimming pool or golf course.

Another attractive aspect of senior planned communities is that the homeowners' association regulates the communities. Hence, an older individual can participate in the creation of the rules and regulations, which in turn are developed to preserve the quality of life of the residents.

Age-segregated communities are a housing option for the older adult who would prefer to live in an apartment or cottage-style house in a planned housing development. The types of housing in this option include apartment buildings, retirement hotels, condominiums, mobile home parks, retirement subdivisions, villages, and even entire towns.

One frequently asked question about these age-restricted communities is whether they are constitutional. This question was resolved in 1988 when Congress amended the Federal Fair Housing Act, which invalidated discrimination based on "family status."

This amendment exempted housing restricted exclusively for the elderly, but it carved out three permissible categories of housing for the elderly:

1. Housing provided under any state or federal program "specifically designed and operated to assist elderly persons."

2. Housing "intended for, and solely occupied by, persons sixty-two years of age or older."

3. Housing "intended and operated for occupancy by persons fifty-five years of age or older."

Supportive housing is a perfect housing option for those older individuals who are plagued by physical frailty, mental decline, or chronic illness but who are basically self-sufficient and value their personal autonomy. The supportive housing setting provides services that can assist elderly individuals in their daily activity; however, these services fall short of providing the care that nursing homes provide. The supportive housing environment may consist of regular meal service, social activities designed to foster continued interaction with one's age peers, transportation to cultural activities, religious outings, recreational outings, readily accessible services such as beauty shops and barbershops, and handy pharmaceutical outlets. (Other accessories include the typical grab bars and other safety features in the restrooms and pull cords or similar alert/alarm systems whose purpose is to ensure the safety of the residents.)

The main producers of the supportive housing project are not-for-profit organizations, such as religious groups. These groups receive subsidies from the federal government. These federal subsidies are usually accompanied by prerequisites. The most commonly seen prerequisites are that the projects be administered by the local public housing administrators and be able to satisfy the low-rent category of housing. The latter of these prerequisites makes these supportive housing communities very appealing to the elderly.

Additionally, older individuals should be aware that their rent can be lowered even more, depending on their financial situation. This reduction in rent can be accredited to "Section 8" rent subsidies. What usually occurs during the Section 8 process is that the federal government pays the difference between the actual rent charged and the market rental rate for that unit. An older individual must be at least sixty-two years old to benefit from this subsidy. The other factor that older adults should be aware of is that his or her income cannot exceed 80% of the median income in the local area, as adjusted for family size. This income includes literally all of the older individual's sources of income.

Nonmedical residential settings can't stop the aging process; they can only delay it by promoting an appropriate lifestyle. Therefore, with illness or poor health, the older individual will likely have to deal with the fact that he or she can no longer safely live alone. This unwelcome dependence on others is where the non-medical residential care facilities come into play. This housing option provides an intermediate level of care, which means it is situated between independent living and the institutional care of nursing homes.

The goal of any assisted-living option is to provide services to older adults who cannot perform daily life activities but who fall short of needing the care of a nursing home. In short, the goal is to provide a quasi-support service while not evading the personal autonomy of the older adult. This goal is accomplished by providing an opportunity to enjoy recreation, social activities, and meals in common areas. The majority of individuals who reside in these assisted-living facilities are single, given that the average married couple can usually care for themselves at their own residence.

Another factor to consider when discussing the assisted-living facility is that these facilities are restricted to admitting only those older individuals who are not bedfast. This particular exemption exists because special needs can be administered or performed only by a licensed nursing home. This policy is in place not only for the protection of the elderly individual who is bedfast but also for the protection of the other residents.

One should keep in mind that there are also temporary assisted-living facilities available. This agreement is done through contracts between the parties. For example, the admissions contract may permit the assisted-living unit to require the resident to move (likely to a nursing home) should the chronic illness become too severe.

Another beneficial aspect of assisted living is that it usually provides a service that aids residents with medication taking, measurements, and dispensing. Additionally the assisted-living facility performs a limited amount of custodial care, which encompasses bathing, grooming, and dressing. Licensed staff will usually perform the above tasks, and they will be on-site and on duty at all times. There is no fixed rate on these assisted-living facilities. The rates usually vary depending on the quality of care and degree of luxury offered.

The financing of these assisted-living facilities is usually dealt with by the proceeds produced by the sale of the older individual's home. This unfortunate financing option is due to the lack of governmental support. However, the individual should confer with his or her state before spending the proceeds from the sale of his or her home, because some states are granted "waivers" on the limits that the government places on Medicare funds.

Additionally, a number of older adults may be able to rely on their long-term insurance to aid in the cost of assisted living. For the purposes of coverage, the long-term insurance policies end up placing assisted-living facilities in the same category as nursing homes. The typical situation that triggers these long-term policies is when the older individual has two or more deficits in their activities of daily living (ADLs).

Moreover, it would be helpful if the contract contained a termination-of-residence clause. Termination in these facilities usually occurs due to death of the resident, voluntary discharge by the resident, or an eviction of the resident due to the resident's deteriorating health.

Current housing trends indicate that there really is no place like home. When asked about their preference for housing, most seniors answer, "What I would really like to do is to stay right here." One's own home represents security and independence to most Americans.

According to a study completed by the American Association of Retired People, 9 out of 10 seniors over the age of seventy live in conventional housing; however, the regular housing stock is not designed to meet their changing needs, tastes, and preferences. Most of the current housing stock is designed for young, active, and mobile people. To live at home, a person must, at the very least, have access to transportation, shop, cook, and do household chores. Many of us will lose one or more of these abilities as we grow older.

Therefore, the future direction of housing, to meet the needs of older persons, will continue in the direction that allows residents to age in place for as long as possible. A brief definition of the phrase *age in place* refers to (1) living where you have lived for many years or (2) living in a non-health-care environment and using products, services, and conveniences to allow or enable you not to have to move as circumstances change. More recently, the term *aging-in-place* has been used in marketing by those in the rapidly evolving senior-housing industry. Continuing-care retirement communities, by definition, offer the chance to age in place, but first the older adult must move to his or her community to "start aging."

Today, multilevel campuses market independent living, assisted living, and perhaps Alzheimer's care and skilled nursing in one location and claim to offer the opportunity to age in place, but again the older adult must move there first. In many cases, older adults must also move from one wing of the campus to another to receive the increased services. Clearly, this option, while better than most, does not satisfy the desire of older adults not to leave their existing homes and their existing neighborhoods.

The future direction of housing to meet the needs of older persons will continue in the direction that allows residents to age in place for as long as possible. The direction needs to focus on allowing older adults to remain in their existing homes. One option available to older adults is to purchase in-home services to cope with declining abilities. For a fee, an army of workers will appear to cut your grass, wash your windows, cook your meals, do the shopping, and even provide personal care and/or skilled nursing care. This may be the best option for a limited number of older adults, depending on the amount of help they need. However, this can be expensive and requires a lot of management and coordination.

Home modification is another option or alternative to relocation, and the promotion of aging-in-place will increase the popularity of programs that modify existing conditions. Home modification and repair programs include adaptations to homes that can make it easier and safer to carry out activities such as bathing, cooking, and climbing stairs, as well as alterations to the physical structure of the home to improve its overall safety and condition.

Home modification and repair can help prevent accidents such as falls. Research suggests that one-third to one-half of home accidents can be prevented by modification and repair.

Home modification and repair can allow people to remain in their homes. Older people tend to live in older homes that often need repairs and modifications. Over 60% of older persons live in homes more than 20 years old. Home modification and repair can accommodate lifestyle changes, increase comfort, and provide an excellent option for older adults to age in place and not have to relocate.

Independent living is an option that offers a lot of versatility. Most elderly enjoy being able to live where they want and do what they want. Independence is often associated with freedom and a person's free will to do what he or she wants. As residents in an independent setting, elderly residents will have more freedom. They won't be classified as people who need assistance, and they cannot rely on a medical infrastructure to provide them with support and care.

Senior apartments are a good choice for older adults who can take care of themselves. Usually, these apartments are developed like standard apartments, but they differ in that they have an age restriction.

Some apartments are also equipped with assistive technology such as handrails and pull cords to aid elderly residents. Overall these apartments are great for a community of elderly neighbors, without the hassles associated with managing a larger home. Considering the research indications that a large percentage of older adults rent rather than own their own home, the popularity of senior apartments will continue to increase both for the private-sector market and as a low-income housing option for older adults.

Independent living differs in medical services offered depending on where the resident lives. Residents generally require no extra assistance with daily tasks. Independent housing includes everything from houses to town houses to apartments. The only factor that makes it different from other housing without medical services is the fact that the elderly residents don't require help. If independent living is part of an established pay community, such as in the case of a CCRC, the services offered to the dependent population are the same ones offered to the independent population, if they choose to use them.

Cooperative Housing - If the word "cooperative" were to be construed narrowly, it may be thought that a cooperative housing development should come into existence only when a group of people, in need of an apartment or home, decide to pool their resources and develop for *themselves* the housing they need. But the great majority of cooperatives began through altruism, not self-help; they began because a group of citizens, full of goodwill, wished to help others get a decent apartment or house at a price they could afford (Liblit, 1964).

Research is extremely sparse in the area of cooperative housing for older adults, and even more so when neighborhood satisfaction variables are added to the mix. One main theme that seems to surface in existing research is that housing cooperatives have been most successful when sponsored and developed by public service agencies. The benefits of this consumer-oriented approach to development are housing costs, quality of construction and design, and smooth operations (Liblit, 1964).

Cooperative housing, as an alternative for older adults, is not limited to the United States. It has made far greater advances in Europe than it has in this country. As the cooperative housing movement grows and new developments come into the picture, the need for exchange of information, review of common problems, and joint action becomes apparent. The National Association of Housing Cooperatives was established in 1950 to serve as a catalyst for cooperative development and to represent and advance the interests of housing cooperatives throughout the country. It represents housing cooperatives, professionals, organizations, and individuals promoting the interests of cooperative housing communities. The association is the only national housing cooperative organization (National Association of Housing Cooperatives, 1993).

Housing cooperatives have succeeded in bringing back the spirit of neighborliness and community that had begun to disappear from many low- and middle-income areas in large urban areas (Liblit, 1964). Cooperatives create feelings of permanence and sociability. According to the National Association of Housing Cooperatives (1993), 3 million people have chosen to live in cooperative housing units in the United States. These housing cooperatives vary from small, family-style homes to large, multistory apartment buildings. They also vary considerably in their equity structures and level of resident involvement. Cooperatives exist for housing of students, older adults, individuals, and families.

Studies conducted on senior housing cooperatives suggest that the participatory nature of cooperatives enhances the quality of life of the residents. Cooperative members showed that participatory management leads to greater satisfaction and well-being among homeowners, particularly those who choose to become involved in the management of their cooperatives (Van Ryzin, 1992).

Age-segregated housing, sometimes referred to as congregate housing, clusters older adults into a single setting, separating them from other age cohorts. Prior to 1980 this concept did not include housing for individuals oriented toward medical care or assisted-living care; it was directed toward older adults in relatively good health who were capable of caring for themselves (Donahue, Thompson, & Curen, 1977; U.S. Department of Housing and Urban Development, 1979; Lawton, 1980). In most cases studied, age-segregated housing included provision of at least some level of service such as dining room for congregate meals, security, lounge areas, laundry facilities, transportation, and hair-care services. Today age-segregated housing is termed the continuing-care retirement community, which will be discussed in greater detail later. The continuing-care retirement community is similar to the age-segregated congregate, but it adds another dimension: a broad or diverse level of care is provided, from independent living to skilled nursing care. Although the social gerontologists and planners of the 1950s and 1960s seemed to feel that age-segregated communities were the answer for the masses of older persons, there is much more realization today that age segregation is by no means for all, or even most, older adults (Lawton, 1977, 1985). Older adults continue to live in the wider, "age-integrated" community because that is where they want to be and are capable of living.

It should be noted that, prior to 1977, virtually every study examining life satisfaction and age-segregated housing concluded that residents of congregate housing find it a very satisfactory housing situation. In general, age-segregated housing seemed to lead to better quality of life. Factors such as independence, friendships, services, and safety often surfaced as high indicators of life satisfaction among the older adult residents in age-segregated housing (Sherman, 1972; Lawton & Cohen, 1974; Carp, 1975; Malozemoff, Anderson, & Rosenbaum, 1977; U.S. Department of Housing and Urban Development, 1979; Chellis, Seagle, & Seagle, 1982; Golant, 1985; Hinrichsen, 1985; and numerous others).

There are some barriers that surfaced with age-segregated housing, or the continuing-care retirement community. They may perpetuate the ageism notion that one is "old" and one is "different." This ageism view is quite pervasive and influenced the image of age-segregated housing such as nursing homes with total institutional quality. Some researchers state that age segregation can reduce the level of activity among adults while reducing independence (Jacobs, 1974; Lawton, 1985). An often neglected factor in age-segregated housing is site placement and neighborhood characteristics that residents reported as important (Wireman & Sebastian, 1986).

Continuing-Care Retirement Communities (CCRCs) are one option in particular that have become extremely popular among non-profit organizations, developers, and older adults. Retirement communities of this type stand out because of the perceived wide-ranging advantages they offer to their residents.

The case study suggests that the future of the continuing-care retirement community built in both rural and suburban locations is uncertain. This case study does not hold any bias toward the concept of providing a continuum of care for older adults. The case study will explain and describe how and why the continuing-care retirement community concept should be an option available for older adults wanting to live in an urban environment during their retirement years.

The continuing-care retirement community concept is rooted in providing older adults within the community with several housing options. Individuals can select the lifestyle that fits with their personal needs. The continuing-care retirement community concept also offers a range of services, amenities, and health and wellness programs - all geared toward helping residents stay healthy and independent for as long as possible. But the foremost advantage that the continuing-care retirement community concept offers is providing residents with access to high-quality assisted-living services and nursing care if required.

The continuum-of-care concept offers residents specialized services, support, and security. Residents derive great peace of mind from knowing that there are three levels of care - all within the same community. They know that if their needs change, the appropriate level of support is available - from independent living to assisted living and nursing care. An ever-increasing number of seniors are choosing to spend their retirement years in a continuing-care retirement community. Nationwide, more than 625,000 retirees make their homes in continuing-care retirement communities. This case study will ask why. One can predict that the continuing-care retirement community is attractive because of the range of housing options and services it provides, the design of age-sensitive housing, and the ease of mobility in an "elderly-friendly" environment.

Continuing-care retirement community residents are supplied with housing, services, and care through the provision of a continuing-care contract (which is also called the "residence and care agreement"). Within the continuing-care industry, there are three types of continuing-care retirement community contracts: extensive, modified, and fee-for-service. While the conditions and terms might vary from one community to the next, a few basic characteristics are common to all communities.

The following explanation of the types of contracts available to residents is based on the Porter Hills Residence and Care Service Contract.

These three contracts differ according to the type of housing, services, amenities, and care provided to the resident. No matter which type of contract the continuing-care retirement community offers, it sets forth the legal and financial agreements between the continuing-care retirement community and the resident. The contract details the accommodations, services, and care the facility is obligated to provide and serves as a protection to residents in that it clearly specifies all terms and conditions of the agreements.

The contract specifically sets forth the financial obligations that new residents are assuming (i.e., the amount of the entrance fee and the amount of the monthly accommodation fee). The contract also includes a cancellation clause that specifies the portion of the fees that shall be refunded if a resident leaves the community.

Of the three types of contracts, the modified contract offers several advantages. It offers residents lower up-front entry fees than extensive contracts, and it offers inclusive nursing care at rates much lower than those offered by fee-for-service contracts. While fee-for-service contracts do offer nursing care, the cost for such care is significantly higher than that provided for with a modified contract.

There are also possible tax benefits to living in a continuing-care retirement community. The United States Internal Revenue Service may recognize a percentage of both the entrance fee and monthly fee as a medical expense deduction. This means that a portion of the entrance fee may be deductible for the year in which residents move in to the community. In addition, the Internal Revenue Service may allow a portion of the monthly fee to be deducted each year, providing residents with an ongoing medical tax deduction. Each year, continuing-care retirement community auditors compute the percentage deduction that the Internal Revenue Services may allow (all computations are subject to IRS rulings). Older adults who are considering a move to a continuing-care retirement community should consult their personal tax adviser for the tax implications of the deduction on their personal tax return.

The current and future housing situation for older adults would not be a great concern if families, friends, and institutions such as churches were able to provide the individualized support that each person needs as he or she ages. But the reality of the aging of the baby boom generation is such that proportionately and numerically, society stands to be overwhelmed by the needs of older adults. The number of people who are sixty-five years of age and older in the United States will more than double between 2000 and 2030, ultimately representing 1 out of every 5 people. It is in our collective best interest, as individuals and as a society, to aggressively address the housing needs of our aging population.

2

When Home Is Not an Option

The gap between the number of affordable housing units and the number of people needing them has created a housing crisis for poor older people. Between 1973 and 1993, over 2 million low-rent units disappeared from the market. These units were abandoned, were converted into condominiums or expensive apartments, or became unaffordable because of cost increases. Between 1991 and 1995, median rental costs paid by low-income renters, the majority of those over the age of sixty-five, rose 21%; at the same time, the number of low-income renters increased.

Over these years, in conjunction with the poor economy, the affordable housing gap grew by 1 million (Daskal, 1998). By 1995, the number of low-income renters in America outstripped the number of low-cost rental units by 4.4 million rental units - the largest shortfall on record (Daskal, 1998). More recently, the strong economy has caused rents to soar, putting housing out of reach for the poorest Americans. Between 1995 and 1997, rents increased faster than income for the 20% of American households with the lowest incomes (U.S. Department of Housing and Urban Development, 1999). This same study found that the number of housing units that rent for less than $300, adjusted for inflation, declined from almost 7 million in 1996 to just below 6 million in 1998, a 20% drop of over 1 million units. The loss of affordable housing puts even greater numbers of people, mainly older adults, at risk of becoming homeless.

As one grows old, the decision of where to live is one of the most difficult challenges to deal with. One of the main contributing factors to the difficult challenge of choosing appropriate housing is the unpredictability of how we will age and how long we will live. In addition to the unpredictability of aging, one must be concerned with the reality that the average life expectancy is increasing, which leads to a higher probability that the elderly of today will have to deal with some sort of chronic health condition. Hence, one's ability to maintain well-being and self-sufficiency while living out one's abridged life tends to become a very expensive goal. This expense has an unfortunate effect on the majority of the elderly, due to the reductions in income after retirement. There are a variety of approaches to aid the elderly in this challenging struggle, and usually the first and most common option exercised is government aid.

In the future, low-income subsidies will need to increase and government aid for elderly housing will need to come in the form of (1) cash subsidy, (2) subsidized home maintenance programs, or (3) a matching service to locate a paying tenant to share an older person's house and help maintain it. While there are programs in place today to support low-income housing subsidies for older adults, there is no government funding on the levels needed to support the increasing number of older adults over the age of sixty-five.

Although the average elderly individual would prefer to remain in his or her original home, frailty, chronic illness, and disability often prevent this dream from ever materializing. When health is in fragile condition (or something like this), the elderly individual's options are limited to some form of assisted housing or institutional settings. The majority of the elderly choose the former over the latter, because service-rich housing presents a far more attractive setting than institutional settings.

Additionally, it should be noted that the elderly who are unable to maintain themselves without the aid of the supportive services are not limited to the choice of a skilled nursing setting. An attractive option for this category of the elderly is a group home setting, which is staffed by qualified personnel that provide nutrition, housekeeping, personal care, and service.

For older adults willing to relocate, there will be improvements to the existing housing options available, although there may be some confusion about what all the terms mean. You may hear about *board-and-care homes, personal care homes, life care facilities,* and *continuing-care retirement facili-*

ties. All refer to some type of "independent living" or "assisted living" or service-oriented housing.

During the 2004 presidential election there was a great deal of discussion around the Social Security crisis, and the debate over the amount of funds available to older adults today and in the future will continue for generations to come. While Social Security has been a long-standing means by which America assists older adults, we as a society have ignored and neglected one area that has a profound impact on the quality of day-to-day living - housing. Politicians and civic leaders continue to ignore the bricks-and-mortar issues associated with aging. Senior housing designed to meet the needs of low-income and middle-income older adults never makes the national agenda and is never mentioned in the State of the Union Address given by the newly elected president.

Americans associate older adults and aging with a Social Security check along with other ageism attitudes and views. Most ageism attitudes, as I will discuss in a later chapter, stem from a lack of knowledge on the part of society as a whole and an inability to educate both young and old on the aging process. The Social Security Act and Older Americans Act were never intended to be a gauge as to when a person has reached old age; rather the Social Security Act and the Older Americans Act were intended to improve the quality of life for older adults and protect against unfair treatment.

The Social Security Act and the Older Americans Act were passed in the same year as Medicare and established the primary vehicle for organizing and delivering community-based services through a coordinated system at the state level. Initially, the Older Americans Act emphasized small grants to state agencies on aging to fund social services programs, such as Passport and RSS. In Ohio, there are 12 area agencies on aging serving Ohio's elderly population. The Western Reserve Area Agency on Aging is the local entity serving 5 northern Ohio counties. Soon after, specific funding was authorized for state planning and coordinating activities.

Through amendments in 1972, a major service component of the national nutrition program for the elderly was added. Beginning in the late 1970s, several trends occurred that shifted the focus of the Older Americans Act activities. Funds became more limited, forcing programs to deal differently with the fact that the aged population is diverse with different levels of need. Particular populations were identified as vulnerable, including frail elders, older women, minorities, rural elders, and the growing number of oldest old individuals.

As the proportion of older frail elderly has increased, the emphasis has shifted from community-based social services for a broad population (such as senior centers, volunteer programs, and recreational activities) to more health-related, long-term care services for the frail elderly who are at risk for institutionalization. Developing a community-based long-term care structure, which was a new concept in the 1980s for most communities, meant significant state and local planning and increased involvement of private and for-profit providers.

In order to better understand what services are offered under the Older Americans Act, it is important to review the objectives and intentions of the Older Americans Act. The following are the objectives of the act:

- Provide adequate income in retirement in accordance with the American standard of living.

- Provide the best possible physical and mental health that science can make available and without regard to economic status.

- Obtain and maintain suitable housing, independently selected, designed and located with reference to special needs and available at costs that older citizens can afford.

- Provide full restoration services for those who require institutional care, and a comprehensive array of community-based, long-term care services adequate to appropriately sustain older people in their communities and in their homes, including support to family members and other persons providing voluntary care to older individuals needing long-term care services.

- Provide opportunity for employment with no discriminatory personnel practices because of age.

- Help older Americans retire in health, honor, and dignity after years of contribution to the economy.

- Participate in and contribute to meaningful activity within the widest range of civic, cultural, educational, training, and recreational opportunities.

- Provide efficient community services, including access to low-cost transportation, which provide a choice in supported living arrangements and social assistance in a coordinated manner and which are readily available when needed, with emphasis on maintaining a continuum of care for vulnerable older individuals.

- Provide immediate benefit from proven research knowledge that can sustain and improve health and happiness.

- Allow older Americans to have freedom, independence, and the free exercise of individual initiative in planning and managing their own lives, full participation in the planning and operation of community-based services and programs provided for their benefit, and protection against abuse, neglect, and exploitation.

The Western Reserve Area Agency on Aging receives the majority of its funds from the Older Americans Act. Last year the state of Ohio received $42 million from the federal government from the Older Americans Act. The Western Reserve Area Agency on Aging received $8 million from the state of Ohio and another $2 million from community block grant funds. The annual budget for the Western Reserve Area Agency on Aging was $10 million. The local agency, the Western Reserve Area Agency, serves almost 400,000 older adults, making it the largest local agency on aging in Ohio.

Services provided by the local agency, with the dollars provided by the federal government, include residential supportive services, congregate meals, home-delivered meals, preventive health, and family caregiver support, to name a few. Funds for all of the services mentioned previously are provided by Title III of the Older Americans Act. Two other important titles under the act are Title VII and Title IV. Dollars available under Title VII are for vulnerable elder rights, a fast-growing concern among health-care professionals and leaders. Dollars available under Title IV are for research, training, and discretionary projects and programs.

The following is a very brief description of the objective and intention of Title VII. Known more commonly as the Vulnerable Elder Rights Protection Title, Title VII was created by the 1992 amendments to the Older Americans Act. It addresses the need for strong advocacy to protect and enhance the basic rights and benefits of vulnerable older people. Through Title VII, Congress refocused the Older Americans Act's original advocacy mission and empowered state agencies on aging to "provide firm leadership...to assure that the rights of older adults are protected." Congress also recognized that while conditions for older persons have improved markedly since 1965, there are many vulnerable older adults who suffer serious deprivation, are denied their basic rights and benefits, and need vigorous advocacy on their behalf. Title VII encourages state agencies to concentrate their advocacy efforts on issues affecting those who are the most socially and economically vulnerable.

Title VII has a dual focus. It brings together and strengthens four existing advocacy programs - Long-Term Care Ombudsman Program; Programs for the Prevention of Abuse, Neglect, and Exploitation; State Elder Rights and Legal Assistance Development Programs; and Insurance/Benefits Outreach, Counseling, and Assistance Programs - and calls for their coordination and linkage within each state. In addition, Title VII calls on state agencies to take a holistic approach to elder rights advocacy by coordinating the four programs and fostering collaboration among programs and other advocates in each state to address at a systems level issues of the highest priority for the most vulnerable elders.

Housing that is well designed, suitably located, and affordable contributes to the ability of older persons to maintain their independence. As such, housing is a crucial factor in determining the financial and emotional well-being of older persons. The future direction of housing needs for older persons will continue in the direction that allows residents to age in place for as long as possible. Therefore, a brief description of what the term aging-in-place means is in order.

The No-Choice Generation includes older homeless men and women, those fifty-five and older who are often invisible in today's society as well as the 58% of the entire population that has an annual income of less than

$20,000. The older homeless generation rarely captures more than a line or two in any text written on the homeless, and when the aging homeless are discussed, they are often represented as old drunks on skid row or as the shopping bag lady slumped on the local park bench. Current public policy focuses implicitly on younger homeless people, for example, mothers with small children. In addition, public policy is overly concerned with social categories in which aging homeless people are subsumed without special notice. The following topical research study is an overview of aging and homelessness in the United States today.

The questions that this topical essay sets out to address are many. However, first it is important to understand the state of homelessness in the United States on a larger scale. Then, with a basic understanding of homelessness in general and the state of homelessness among older adults, we can begin to answer the following questions:

- Who are elderly homeless people in the United States?
- What are the causes of homelessness?
- What are the public policies to help the elderly homeless?
- What are the consequences of homelessness?

Retirement in poverty and homelessness are inextricably linked. Poor people are frequently unable to pay for housing, food, child care, health care, and education. Difficult choices must be made when limited resources cover only some of these necessities. Often it is housing that absorbs a high proportion of income that must be dropped. Being poor means being an illness, or an accident, away from living on the streets.

In 1997, over 13% of the United States population, equal to over 35 million people, lived in poverty. In addition, according to the 1998 United States Bureau of the Census data, 14 million people, or approximately 41% of all poor persons, had incomes of less than half the poverty level. This represents an increase of over 500,000 people from 1995. Forty percent of persons living in poverty are children; in fact, the 1997 poverty rate of 20% for children is almost twice as high as the poverty rate for any other age group.

Two factors help account for increasing poverty: eroding employment opportunities for large segments of the workforce, including those over the age of fifty-five, and the declining value and availability of public assistance.

Between 1980 and 1993, the total number of older households in the United States, that is, households headed by someone over the age of sixty-five, increased by 31% (Gaberlavage & Sloan, 1997). Among this growing population are older adults who have grown old on the street, those who have recently become homeless, and others at risk of displacement from their homes.

Definitions of aged status vary from study to study; however, there is a growing consensus that persons aged fifty and over should be included in the "older homeless" category. Homeless persons between the ages of fifty and sixty-five frequently fall between the cracks: they are not old enough to receive Medicare, but their physical health, aggravated by poor nutrition and severe living conditions, may resemble that of a person seventy years old.

A 1992 Urban Institute study found that 31% of homeless persons were over the age of forty-five (Burt, 1992); other studies have found proportions of homeless persons between the ages of fifty-five and sixty ranging from just over 2% to close to 20% (Institute of Medicine, 1988). Although the proportion of older persons among the homeless population has declined over the past 2 decades, their absolute number has grown (Cohen, 1996).

Causes of homelessness in later years result from many factors. Increased homelessness among elderly persons is largely the result of the declining availability of affordable housing and poverty among certain segments of the aging. Of the over 12 million persons in households identified by the U.S. Department of Housing and Urban Development as having "worst-case housing needs," about 1 million are elderly people (U.S. Department of Housing and Urban Development, 1998). Among households with very low incomes, households with an elderly head of household have almost a one-in-three chance of having worst-case needs, despite the fact that housing assistance has been heavily directed toward elderly people. Thirty-seven percent of very-low-income elderly people receive housing assistance.

The total number of elderly persons with very low incomes dropped between 1993 and 1995 by about 300,000 (U.S. Department of Housing and Urban Development, 1998). This drop may reflect a growing portion of the elderly population protected from severe poverty by Social Security and private pensions. A recent analysis of U.S. census data found that without Social Security, nearly 50% of Americans aged sixty-five or over would have been poor in 1997 (Center on Budget and Policy Priorities, 1999). In fact, Social Security reduced the poverty rate among elderly people in 1997 by almost 12% and lifted over 11 million elderly people out of poverty.

Still, many elderly people are poor and in need of housing assistance. While elderly people have a lower poverty rate than the general population (about 10% compared to over 13% for all people), they are more likely than the non-elderly to have incomes just over the poverty threshold (United States Bureau of the Census, 1998). Seventeen percent of elderly people had family incomes below 125% of poverty. Sixty-five percent of older renters, 71% of older single female renters, 71% of older Hispanic renters, and 69% of older African-American renters spend more than 30% of their income on housing (Gaberlavage & Citro, 1997).

With less income for other necessities such as food, medicine, and health care, these populations are particularly vulnerable to homelessness. Overall economic growth will not alleviate the income and housing needs of elderly poor people, as continuing or returning to work or gaining income through marriage are often unlikely.

Isolation also contributes to homelessness among older persons; older persons are almost twice as likely as younger homeless persons to have been living alone prior to losing their home (Cohen, 1996).

The consequences of retiring with no home or being homeless has serious consequences for the older adult as well as for society as a whole. Once on the street, older adults often find getting around difficult, and, distrusting the crowds at shelters and clinics, they are more likely to sleep on the street. Some studies show that homeless persons who are elderly are prone to victimization and more likely to be ignored by law enforcement. A study from Detroit, for example, found that almost half of older homeless persons had been robbed and one-fourth had been assaulted within the preceding year (Douglass, 1988). Older homeless persons are also more likely to suffer from a variety of health problems, including chronic disease, functional disabilities, and high blood pressure, than are other homeless persons (Cohen, 1996).

Only a small proportion of local, state, and federal funds for homeless service users are older adults despite public perceptions that homeless people are often elderly. For example, homeless people often appear older than they are due to poor health and harsh living conditions. Elderly homeless people are predominantly single, male, and often in frail health. They have usually lost contact with family and are unlikely to raise problems with landlords due to fear of eviction.

Many older adults are at risk of becoming homeless, as their housing tenure is insecure and the cost of their housing is not consistent with their ability to pay. Elderly women at risk of homelessness are most often in this category. Other common characteristics of elderly people who are homeless or at risk of homelessness include the absence of a friend or relative who could assist in accessing services, a history of long-term private renting, considering themselves undeserving, little or no prior usage of community services, poor health and nutrition, and little knowledge or understanding of community care services.

A lack of affordable housing appropriate to the needs of older adults and a lack of sufficient income to maintain an adequate standard of living are the two predominant causal factors of elderly homelessness. The upgrading of private hotels for tourist accommodation and the popularity of inner-city living have reduced the amount of affordable housing in the inner city (HAAG, 1997, p. 3), whereas new housing rarely suits the needs of elderly people. Investors develop high-cost rental housing and often evict long-term elderly tenants so that they can refurbish existing housing or build new housing that will bring in higher rents.

The loss of social networks and support is also a strong contributing factor for elderly homelessness. As their partners die and elderly people lose touch with their families and friends due to ill health or not wanting to be a burden, elderly people may lose access to those who have provided a traditional caring role and become socially isolated.

There is a lack of access to generalist aged care services for severely financially disadvantaged people, including homeless people. Homeless people cannot afford entry fees to residential care and must compete with those who are wealthier but still within the official threshold of financial disadvantage (as designated by Commonwealth Government aged care services). The culture of aged care services often does not suit homeless people. Most aged care services are available only to those aged sixty-five and over, while it is generally recognized that homeless people age prematurely and may need such services at a younger age than the general population.

Current programs and public policies to support the aging homeless population of men and women have been filled with many false starts and stops. On December 17, 2002, the United States Department of Housing and Urban Development (HUD) announced the award of a record $1 billion in homeless assistance funding to states and localities as part of the agency's homeless "Continuum of Care." These funds were appropriated by Congress as part of the McKinney-Vento Homeless Assistance Act and are directed at the state and local level for permanent supportive housing, emergency shelter grants, and services for homeless individuals and families. Among the permanent supportive housing programs funded under McKinney-Vento are key resources directed to homeless individuals with severe mental illnesses and co-occurring substance abuse disorders, such as Shelter Plus Care and the SHP supportive housing program.

At the state and local level, homeless funds are allocated through the "Continuum of Care," and the planning process is designed to help states and communities prioritize needs of their homeless population. The U.S. Department of Housing and Urban Development then awards funds to these "Continuum of Care" applicants.

Section 8 Vouchers for People with Disabilities announced that in addition to awarding funds for homeless assistance, the U.S. Department of Housing and Urban Development has also released more than $90 million in funding for rental vouchers targeted solely to non-elderly people with disabilities and including adults with severe mental illnesses. These 2002 funding awards announced by the U.S. Department of Housing and Urban Development come in the form of rent subsidies that are administered by local housing authorities (and in some cases, non-profit disability organizations). For each of these programs, housing authorities (and in some cases, state housing agencies and non-profits) apply directly to the U.S. Department of Housing and Urban Development in order to access funds and then administer assistance at the local level. Interested individual consumers, family members, case managers, and others should therefore refer to these referenced awardee lists to determine which local programs in a given state or community have received funding in 2002.

Below is a description of the three separate allocations of tenant-based rental vouchers for people with disabilities and in some cases elderly persons with or without disabilities.

The Section 811 Mainstream program consists of tenant-based rental vouchers that are set aside specifically for people with disabilities. Since 1997, Congress has allowed the United States Department of Housing and Urban Development to transfer up to 25% of the overall Section 811 program away from capital advances/project-based assistance to tenant-based vouchers. Rental vouchers enable recipients to get apartments by paying generally no more than 30% of their monthly income for rent, and the voucher from the U.S. Department of Housing and Urban Development pays the remainder.

Traditionally, only housing authorities have been able to apply directly to the U.S. Department of Housing and Urban Development to receive and administer vouchers at the local level; eligible low-income households (including individuals) apply to housing authorities to get vouchers. However, in the Section 811 Mainstream voucher program, non-profit disability organizations have been able to apply, both this year and last year. NAMI pushed hard to ensure that non-profit disability groups can apply - both to ensure that adults with severe mental illnesses are not discriminated against and to keep 811 as a program focused on non-profits that have a better understanding of the housing and community support needs of people with severe disabilities.

In 2002, the United States Department of Housing and Urban Development awarded just over $50 million in funds for the Section 811 Mainstream program. Several non-profit organizations with expertise in serving adults with severe mental illnesses received Section 811 Mainstream funding in 2002, including Mental Health Resources, Inc., of Minnesota and Transitional Services of Long Island, New York.

In the early 1990s, Congress passed legislation that permits HUD-assisted housing providers to limit or exclude people with disabilities from living in certain subsidized housing developments by designating that housing as "elderly only." These housing developments contain virtually all of the studio and one-bedroom federally subsidized housing units in the country and represent over two-thirds of the federally subsidized housing resources that low-income people with disabilities were eligible to access prior to the passage of this legislation. Non-elderly individuals with severe mental illnesses have been particularly disadvantaged in many communities across the country as private owners of assisted housing have changed tenant selection policies to exclude people with disabilities.

Since 1997, Congress has funded tenant-based vouchers to make up the loss of assisted housing for which non-elderly people with disabilities could apply. For the fiscal year of 2002, the U.S. Department of Housing and Urban Development allocated $20 million for the "certain developments" pot of vouchers. Unlike the Section 811 Mainstream voucher program, only local public housing authorities are able to apply for this "certain developments" allocation of Section 8 vouchers for people with disabilities. Because the U.S. Department of Housing and Urban Development and applicant public housing authorities have very limited capacity to track which private owners of assisted housing have shifted their tenant selection policies since 1993 to disfavor non-elderly people with disabilities, the agency has experienced difficulties in allocating funds for these vouchers. (Note: For 3 years, the United States Department of Housing and Urban Development has failed to conduct a congressionally mandated inventory of which properties have shifted to "elderly only.")

As a result, the U.S. Department of Housing and Urban Development has been able to fund all eligible applications from public housing authorities for this funding. Thus, the chances of a public housing authority being awarded this funding are very good. Because of the extremely low number of public housing authority applicants, each year there has been money left over after all of the qualifying applications were awarded, signaling to the disability community that more pressure needs to be put on local public housing authorities to educate them about this funding opportunity. The money that is left in this "pot" after awards have been made is then rolled into the Section 811 Mainstream program, described above, but is only available to PHA applicants as one-year grants and not to nonprofit disability organizations. This is another reason why nonprofit disability organizations who are interested in administering Section 811 Mainstream vouchers may choose to engage in a partnership with a public housing authority, since public housing authorities have a better chance of being funded.

But what is being done to help the homeless elderly population? Most older homeless persons are entitled to Social Security benefits; however, these benefits are often inadequate to cover the cost of housing. In 1998, on a national average, a person receiving Supplemental Security Income benefits had to spend 69% of his or her monthly Supplemental Security Income to rent a one-bedroom apartment at fair market rent; in more than 125 housing market areas, the cost of a one-bedroom apartment at fair market rent was more than a person's total monthly Supplemental Security Income (Technical Assistance Collaborative & the Consortium for Citizens with Disabilities Housing Task Force, 1999). In most states, even if the Supplemental Security Income grant does cover the rent, only a few dollars remain for other expenses. Moreover, some homeless persons are unaware of their own eligibility for public assistance programs and face difficulties applying for and receiving benefits. Elderly homeless persons in particular often need help navigating the complex application process.

Recently, in Milwaukee, a church was declared a public nuisance for feeding elderly homeless people and allowing them to sleep there. In Gainesville, police threatened University of Florida students with arrest if they did not stop serving meals to elderly homeless people in a public park. In Santa Barbara, it is illegal to lean against the front of a building or store, and no one can park a motor home on the street in one place for more than 2 hours.

These ordinances and activities demonstrate the increasingly hostile attitude in the United States toward older people who are homeless, according to a report by the National Coalition for the Homeless that was released recently. This report examines occurrences since January 2002 and documents civil rights violations perpetrated against people experiencing homelessness. With the highest unemployment rates in almost a decade, more older adults are becoming homeless, and as the economy continues to tighten, it is causing financial crises for shelters and service-providing agencies. Though nearly all cities still lack sufficient shelter beds and social services, many continue to pass laws prohibiting people experiencing homelessness from sleeping outside.

Almost 70% of the cities surveyed in a recent report have passed at least one or more new laws specifically targeting older homeless people since January 2002, making it increasingly difficult to survive on the streets. Cities are attempting to make it illegal to perform life-sustaining activities in public, while at the same time refusing to allocate sufficient funds to address the causes of homelessness.

The National Homeless Civil Rights Organizing Project (NHCROP), a project of the National Coalition for the Homeless comprised of local advocates in communities across the country, has compiled quantitative and qualitative data samplings from 147 communities in 42 states, Puerto Rico, and the District of Columbia. These cities represent rural, urban, and suburban areas in all geographic and demographic varieties.

"Instead of the compassionate responses that communities have used to save lives in the past 2 decades, the common response to homelessness is to criminalize the victims through laws and ordinances that make illegal life-sustaining activities that people experiencing homelessness are forced to do in public," said Donald Whitehead, Executive Director of the National Coalition for the Homeless, who was himself formerly homeless.

As it becomes increasingly difficult to afford housing, this country is turning to jails instead of creating affordable housing by enacting the Bringing America Home Act (H.R. 2897 - 108th Congress). These individuals and families are arrested for committing such illegal acts as sitting or standing on sidewalks and napping in parks. Whitehead stated, "At the national level, we see a relationship between municipalities' efforts to make homelessness a crime and the increases in hate crimes and violent acts directed at homeless people in those cities."

Brian Davis, Executive Director of the Northeast Ohio Coalition for the Homeless, said, "Imagine the loneliness and feeling of helplessness, when every shelter is full and then the city's police force adds insult to injury by confiscating all your belongings or issues a ticket for sleeping in a park. It takes a special person to be able to cope with the daily struggle to survive while the city government throws added barriers into your path toward stability."

In summary, the gap between the number of affordable housing units and the number of people needing them has created a housing crisis for poor older people. Between 1973 and 1993, over 2 million low-rent units disappeared from the market. These units were abandoned, were converted into condominiums or expensive apartments, or became unaffordable because of cost increases. Between 1991 and 1995, median rental costs paid by low-income renters, the majority of those over the age of sixty-five, rose 21%; at the same time, the number of low-income renters increased. Over these years, in conjunction with the poor economy, the affordable housing gap grew by 1 million (Daskal, 1998).

By 1995, the number of low-income renters in America outstripped the number of low-cost rental units by 4.4 million rental units - the largest shortfall on record (Daskal, 1998). More recently, the strong economy has caused rents to soar, putting housing out of reach for the poorest Americans. Between 1995 and 1997, rents increased faster than income for the 20% of American households with the lowest incomes (U.S. Department of Housing and Urban Development, 1999). This same study found that the number of housing units that rent for less than $300, adjusted for inflation, declined from almost 7 million in 1996 to just below 6 million in 1998, a 20% drop of over 1 million units. The loss of affordable housing puts even greater numbers of people, mainly older adults, at risk of becoming homelessness.

The lack of affordable housing has led to high rent burdens (rents that absorb a high proportion of income), overcrowding, and substandard housing. These phenomena, in turn, have not only forced many people to become homeless but also put a large and growing number of people at risk of becoming homeless. A recent study by the United States Housing and Urban Development office found that over 5 million unassisted, very-low-income older households had "worst-case needs" for housing assistance in 1995 (U.S. Department of Housing and Urban Development, 1998). This figure is an all-time high and represents an 8% increase over the 1989 figure.

Housing assistance can be the difference between stable housing, precarious housing, or no housing at all. However, the demand for assisted housing clearly exceeds the supply: only about one-third of poor renter households receive a housing subsidy from the federal, the state, or a local government (Daskal, 1998). The limited level of housing assistance means that most poor families and individuals seeking housing assistance are placed on long waiting lists. From 1996 to 1998, the time households spent on waiting lists for HUD housing assistance grew dramatically. For the largest public housing authorities, a family's average time on a waiting list rose from 22 to 33 months from 1996 to 1998, which is equal to a 50% increase (U.S. Department of Housing and Urban Development, 1999). The average waiting period for a Section 8 rental assistance voucher rose from 26 months to 28 months between 1996 and 1998. Excessive waiting lists for public housing mean that older poor people must remain in shelters or inadequate housing arrangements longer. Consequently, there is less shelter space available for other homeless people, who must find shelter elsewhere or live on the streets.

A housing trend with a particularly severe impact on aging homelessness is the loss of single-room-occupancy housing. In the past, single-room-occupancy housing served to house many poor individuals, including poor older persons suffering from mental illness or substance abuse. From 1970 to the mid-1980s, an estimated 1 million single-room-occupancy housing units were demolished (Dolbeare, 1996). The demolition of single-room-occupancy housing was most notable in large cities:

between 1970 and 1982, New York City lost 87% of its $200-per-month-or-less single-room-occupancy housing stock; Chicago experienced the total elimination of cubicle hotels; and by 1985, Los Angeles had lost more than half of its downtown single-room-occupancy housing (Koegel et al., 1996). From 1975 to 1988, San Francisco lost 43% of its stock of low-cost residential hotels; from 1970 to 1986, Portland, Oregon, lost 59% of its residential hotels; and from 1971 to 1981, Denver lost 64% of its single-room-occupancy hotels (Wright & Rubin, 1997). Thus the destruction of single-room-occupancy housing is a major factor in the growth of homelessness in many cities.

Finally, it should be noted that the largest federal housing assistance program is the entitlement to deduct mortgage interest from income for tax purposes. In fact, for every $1 spent on low-income housing programs, the federal treasury loses $4 to housing-related tax expenditures, 75% of which benefit households in the top fifth of income distribution (Dolbeare, 1996). Moreover, in 1994 the top fifth of households received 61% of all federal housing benefits (tax and direct), while the bottom fifth received only 18%. Thus, federal housing policy has not responded to the needs of low-income households, while disproportionately benefiting the wealthiest Americans.

To prevent elderly Americans from becoming homeless, we must provide enough low-income housing, income supports, and health-care services to sustain independent living. For those older adults who have already lost their homes, comprehensive outreach health and social services must be made available, as well as special assistance to access existing public assistance programs. Finally, like all people who are homeless or at risk of becoming homeless, elderly people need an adequate income, affordable housing, and affordable health care in order to stay securely housed.

3

Relocation in Later Years

There is no place like home - it is a term and a concept easily taken for granted. Few would find fault with the sentiment it expresses. However, if thoughtfully addressed to the needs of an aging society, it begins to take on far greater significance. Hidden deep in this simple cliché are implications of comfort, security, family, friendships, happiness, and independence. Unfortunately, today those simple words are at the center of national and local debates over the state of the nation's housing for an increasing older adult population.

According to the 2000 United States census and the National Center on Health Statistics, approximately 12% of all noninstitutionalized older adults lived alone. The percentage of women living alone was substantially higher than that of men. Even more significant perhaps is the fact that the number of older persons living alone increased by 13% between 1970 and 2000, about one and one-half times the growth rate for the older population in general (AARP & AOA, 2003). The combined total of older adults, both men and women over the age of sixty-five, either living alone or living with a family member or a spouse will increase to 70 million people by the year 2030.

In recent years, the focus in the area of housing for older adults has been on maintaining what already exists and making better use of existing housing resources through home sharing, accessory apartments, and home equity conversions. The previous trend was to meet older people's housing needs through adapting existing communities and neighborhoods rather than through expensive housing programs (Newcomer, Lawton, & Byerts, 1986).

The housing requirements for older adults are significantly different from the requirements of young adults, due to the progressive limitations of mobility, physical, social, and mental characteristics of older adults over time (Golant, 1992). This creates needs and demands that seem to conflict with the ability to maintain an active life.

Community-dwelling older adults who move gracefully to retirement communities tend to be pragmatic planners who see the change as a necessary new beginning (Blank, 1988; Brand & Smith, 1974). Much of the following review of literature relating to the question of why older adults move to communities boasting of better retirement characteristics supports the theory that older adults want to make their own decisions, relieve their relatives of responsibility, and eliminate worry about future health and home care. Consequently, they reap new freedom to pursue activities they love, new friends and often better health (Bull, 1993).

But this may not be the case with the new generation of older adults. Research indicates that the current Multiple-Choice Generation is wealthier and healthier than past generations. Does more money and better health affect the decision of older adults to relocate in later years?

The following literature review addresses the factors involved in the decision-making process of older adults. The review begins with a brief overview of the theorist Ponsioen (1962), who suggests that a society's first responsibility is to meet the basic survival needs of its members, including biological, social, emotional, and spiritual components.

Each society, or the dominant group in each society, identifies a quality-of-life level below which no individual or group should fall. These levels will change over time. Within this framework, social needs exist when some communities have a service or opportunity and other communities do not.

In contrast to Ponsioen, Maslow (1968) took a slightly different view and proposed the existence of a hierarchy of needs. According to Maslow, an individual becomes aware of needs in a prescribed order from the lower level of a pyramid progressing upward. Only when the lower needs are satisfied can a higher need be addressed. A person cannot be overly concerned with safety and security until physiological survival needs of food and shelter are met. Only when all levels of needs are achieved can attention be directed to the need for love and self-actualization. The need for achievement is manifested in the individual's tendency to strive to accomplish particular tasks in order to generate personal satisfaction and contentment (Maslow, 1987). It involves continued struggle for knowledge and skills and for exploration and mastery of the environment. Older adults exhibit a need for self-esteem or self-actualization to exercise their influence about later life.

Addressing the concerns of these early theorists has yielded a number of useful insights to assessing the needs of older adults. The needs of our aging society are diverse because of the very nature of the aging process and because of the diverse profile of the older population. Life-span studies suggest that older people are more unlike each other than younger people. Not only do people become more different from each other as they age, but there are significant differences among the older adults in this population called aging. The young-old, around sixty-five years old, are quite different from the old-old, eighty-five and older, in personality, health, vigor, and emotional stability. Therefore, addressing the quality of life and basic needs of all older adults demands a clear understanding of the diverse physical, mental, social, and environmental attributes of the individuals in later life (Altman, Lawton, & Wohlwill, 1984).

For the purpose of this research case study, the housing preferences and degree of neighborhood satisfaction of older adults will vary with each particular age group studied. For example, are the participants married or never married, are they male or female, are they at a low socioeconomic level or a high socioeconomic level, do they have a high school education or no high school education, do they have children or do they not have children? Furthermore, the older adults in the current population are healthier, better educated, more active, and more involved in community leadership roles than their counterparts 25 years ago and will probably be just as different from those in the year 2020 (Stevens-Long & Commons, 1992).

The subsequent theories of the 1950s and 1960s help describe why older adults respond to situations as they do; they explain the reasons older adults choose particular housing options. The two specific aging theories addressed below are the disengagement theory and the activist theory. The disengagement theory (Cumming & Henry, 1961) proposed that elderly persons were happiest and most successful when they acknowledged their declining capacities and began to look more and more toward the end of life. It was felt that time and the declining pool of energy were best spent in roles that were specifically different from other age-based roles and unique to old age (grandparenting and great-grandparenting) and in preparation for death. To enable older persons to do these things without guilt and to allow society to fill their former roles with younger, stronger workers and role fillers, disengagement theorists felt it would be best to have older persons segregated so that they could concentrate on their distinct needs and thoughts.

Many gerontological researchers and practitioners were opposed to the implications of the disengagement theory that older people were on the other side of some distinct discontinuity from their pasts and from other age groups (Rose, 1965; Rosow, 1967; Havighurst, Newgarten, & Tobin, 1968). Particularly, they were disturbed about the negativity of the view of old age as little more than a time of waiting to die and the implication that older persons were incompetent to continue to be involved in the roles they had formerly filled so well (Havighurst, Newgarten, & Tobin, 1968).

Theorists opposing disengagement foundations felt that society had done little to provide the alternative roles that would be so important in society, instead leaving older adults with "un-meaningful" roles (Rosow, 1967). These social gerontologists felt that healthy older persons want to continue to live, act, and perform roles quite similarly to what they had done as younger persons. This premise was referred to as activity theory, postulating that the best way to age successfully is to stay active and involved (Havighurst, Newgarten, & Tobin, 1968).

While known for their competing philosophies, both emphasize the magnitude of having roles to fill, specific activities and statuses in society that mark one as "worthwhile" (Lemon, Bengston, & Peterson, 1972; Schaie & Willis, 1986). The two theories, however, proposed diverse ways to ensure that older adults felt valuable in the roles they assumed. Both disengagement and activity theories lend support to the cooperative housing concept but for different reasons.

Disengagement theorists may view cooperative living as a place where older persons would do distinctively different things from younger persons and perform a set of unique roles. It may be promoted as a setting to ensure a continuity of roles for older persons and be seen as a way to enhance roles and activities of older persons. Encouraging a person to move into a totally different housing situation might appear to be an ineffective way to provide continuity with one's past life. There is, however, a logic to it. That logic is rooted in an ageism belief that activity theory shares with disengagement theory that older persons are less able than younger adults to compete for and fill the wide variety of roles needed and valued by our society.

Activity theorists agree that if older persons remain living and working alongside others, they would suffer because the leadership roles and central roles of society would be handed over to younger persons. Cooperative housing would provide new opportunities to fulfill the same kind of roles as before without having to compete with those of other age groups. As older adults age, they become more peripheral, less pivotal actors as the number of settings in which they are involved diminish (Barker & Barker, 1961).

What is particularly interesting about the background of the disengagement and activity theories is that these two major theories about successful aging do not share many similarities but both lend support to the concept of cooperative living and the social importance of the growing aging population. In the 1950s and 1960s, when American society was ready to address some of the big issues about how to assist older adults and ensure their successful aging, disengagement and activity theorists were ready with answers. The answer was to provide age-segregated settings where older persons could congregate as a unit, become an important voting block, and fulfill all their needs. Simultaneously, their withdrawal from the main society allowed their essential roles and positions in society to be available to members of more recent birth cohorts (Rose, 1965; Messer, 1967; Schooler, 1969). Contrary to the disengagement theory, this proposed research study will explain that today, with a rapidly growing population of older adults reaching the age of sixty-five, age-segregated housing may not make sense.

In addition, the disengagement theory does not support or make provisions for those older adults who wish to stay in their existing home in their existing neighborhood and age in place.

The theoretical perspectives on rural and urban differences among older adults have been the focus of several research studies. Many researchers have studied several sociological frameworks addressing rural and urban differences. Considering the current senior housing trend to locate the retiree-dominated, age-segregated community in rural areas, it is important for this study to establish and define rural versus urban differences. The conceptual frameworks discussed in this section are (1) classical theory, (2) determinist theory, (3) compositional theory, and (4) subcultural theory.

Classical theory (Toennies, 1957) focuses on the concept of a societal continuum separated into two basic kinds of social relationships or two ways in which people relate to each other - *gemeinschaft* (community) and *gesellschaft* (society). Gemeinschaft is defined as a sense of mutuality, common destiny, common bond, and obligation. In contrast, gesellschaft identifies the means-to-an-end relationship where each individual is serving his own personal interest. Toennies (1957) felt that both relationships most commonly existed at the same time, but gemeinschaft best characterized the small rural community and the latter was more prevalent in the city.

Determinist theory (Fischer, 1976) debates that urbanism increases the risk or occurrence of social disorders. These psychological factors and social structural changes encourage social disorganization and disintegration (e.g., crime, mental health). Conversely, rural residents in secure communities are less likely to encounter such problems.

Compositional theory (Fischer, 1976) denounces the effects of urbanism and credits the rural-urban differences to the formation of the different populations. Compositionalists do not believe, as their determinist counterpart, that urbanism weakens small, primary groups. They argue that ecological factors, such as size, density, and heterogeneity, do not have important repercussions for personal social structures. Instead, this theory proclaims that non-ecological factors, such as social class, ethnicity, and life stage, influence the dynamics of social life. Financial status, cultural characteristics, and marital/family structure are the primary factors that form an individual's behavior. Subcultural theory (Fischer, 1976) compromises both the determinist and compositional concepts. It believes that urbanism independently affects social life by helping to create and strengthen these social groups. City populations allow the development of such groups as delinquents, professional criminals, and alternative lifestyles, and it is the members of these groups who interact with and support each other (Davensport & Davensport, 1984). Therefore, in contrast to the determinist's view of discouraging social groups, subcultural theory argues that urbanism encourages social groups or subcultures.

Each theoretical orientation falls into the evolutionary continuum of sociology. With the improved communication and transportation systems, urban and rural differences are less pronounced. Both ecological and non-ecological factors are important determinants of behavior. Researchers conclude that caution should be taken when supporting a theory because differences will occur in conceptualizing an outcome in the controversy of rural versus urban (Ponsiaen, 1962; Schulz & Brenned, 1977; Davensport & Davensport, 1984; Stevens-Long & Commons, 1992).

Ageism attitudes among American society have been described as maintaining a stereotypical and often negative perception of older adults (Busse, 1968). This negative and/or stereotypical perception of aging and aged individuals is readily apparent in such areas as language, media, humor, and housing. For example, such commonly used phrases as "over the hill" and "don't be an old fuddy-duddy" denote old age as a period of impotency and incompetence (Nuessel, 1982). The term used to describe this stereotypical and often negative bias against older adults is "ageism" (Butler, 1969). Ageism can be defined as "any attitude, action, or institutional structure which subordinates a person or group because of age or any assignment of roles in society purely on the basis of age" (Traxler, 1980, p. 4). As an "ism," ageism reflects a prejudice in society against older adults. Ageism, however, is different from other "isms" (sexism, racism, etc.) for primarily two reasons. First, age classification is not static. An individual's age classification changes as one progresses through the life cycle. Thus, age classification is characterized by continual change, while the other classification systems traditionally used by society such as race and gender remain constant. Second, no one is exempt from at some point achieving the status of old and therefore, unless they die at an early age, experiencing ageism. The latter is an important distinction, as ageism can thus affect the individual on two levels. First, the individual may be ageist with respect to others. That is, she or he may stereotype other people on the basis of age. Second, the individual may be ageist with respect to self. Thus, ageist attitudes may affect the self-concept. Much research has been conducted concerning ageism. However, the empirical evidence is inconclusive. Some research demonstrates the existence of ageist attitudes (Golde & Kogan, 1959; Kastenbaum & Durkee, 1964a, 1964b; Tuckman & Lorge, 1953) and other research does not (Brubaker & Powers, 1976; Schonfield, 1985). This discrepancy is most likely the result of methodological differences and, in particular, methodological errors. A brief discussion of the major methodological errors or problems found in ageism research may be helpful in clarifying this point. The first major problem is that the majority of ageism research suffers from a mono-method bias. In other words, each study used only one method to operationally define the ageism construct. Methods commonly used have included sentence completion (Golde & Kogan, 1959), semantic differential (Kogan & Wallach, 1961; Rosencranz & McNevin, 1969), Likert scales (Kilty & Feld, 1976), and adjective checklists (Aaronson, 1966). The problem inherent in the use of a mono-method is that any effect found may be an artifact of the method employed rather than the construct under study. Thus, a researcher should employ more than one method to look for consistency in the results.

Another problem, according to Kogan (1979), is the use of within-subject designs in ageism research. In other words, a subject will be asked to complete a questionnaire regarding both younger and older adults. Kogan asserts that by using this methodology, age is pushed to the foreground of a subject's mind. The subject thus becomes aware that the researcher is looking for age differences. Therefore, age differences are found.

The use of primarily younger populations to study ageism represents another problem with ageism research. The majority of ageism research uses children, adolescents, or young adults as subjects and examines their perception of older adults. Only a few studies have examined the perceptions of the population whom the construct affects most - older adults. Those studies which have used an older subject population have unfortunately used primarily institutionalized individuals as subjects (Kastenbaum & Durkee, 1964a; Tuckman & Lavell, 1957). Therefore, they do not represent the vast majority of older adults.

Another problem with much of ageism research is that it only examines the negative stereotypes of old age. More recent studies have suggested that while attitudes toward the aged are increasingly positive, they are still stereotypical (Austin, 1985). Therefore, ageism has been expanded to include positive stereotypical images. However, these are rarely studied (Brubaker & Powers, 1976).

Two additional problems are primarily theoretical in nature. First, ageism research rarely examines or attempts to understand the causes of ageism. Thus, while much theoretical work has been conducted concerning the factors contributing to ageism, little empirical research has been conducted in this area. Second, ageism research rarely examines the interaction between ageism and other "isms." As many individuals are in a position to experience more than one prejudice, the interaction between these prejudices needs to be examined.

The theoretical basis of ageism consists of a negative bias or stereotypical attitude toward aging and the aged. It is maintained in the form of primarily negative stereotypes and myths concerning the older adult. Traxler (1980) outlines four factors that have contributed to this negative image of aging. Each will be discussed below. The first factor that is postulated to contribute to ageism is the fear of death in Western society. Western civilization conceptualizes death as outside of the human life cycle (Butler & Lewis, 1977). As such, death is experienced and viewed as an affront to the self. Death is not seen as a natural and inevitable part of the life course.

This can be contrasted with Eastern philosophy where life and death are all part of a continuous cycle. Death and life are inextricably woven together and the "self" continues throughout. To be a person in Western society, however, means that one must be alive and in control of the events of one's life. Therefore, death is feared.

As death is feared, old age is feared; death and old age are viewed as synonymous in American society (Kastenbaum, 1979). Kastenbaum (1973) hypothesizes that ageism attitudes and stereotypes serve to insulate the young and middle-aged from the ambivalence they feel toward the elderly. This ambivalence results from the fact that the older adult is viewed as representing aging and death. Butler (1969) states, "Ageism reflects a deepseated uneasiness on the part of the young and middle-aged - a personal revulsion to and distaste for growing old, disease, disability; and a fear of powerlessness, 'uselessness,' and death" (p. 243). This represents the most commonly argued basis for ageism.

The second factor postulated by Traxler (1980) to contribute to ageism is the emphasis on the youth culture in American society. For example, the media, ranging from television to novels, place an emphasis on youth, physical beauty, and sexuality. Older adults are primarily ignored or portrayed negatively (Martel, 1968; Northcott, 1975). The emphasis on youth affects not only how older individuals are perceived but also how older individuals perceive themselves. Persons who are dependent on physical appearance and youth for their identity are likely to experience loss of self-esteem with age (Block, Davidson, & Grumbs, 1981).

The emphasis on productivity represents the third factor contributing to ageism in American culture (Traxler, 1980). It should be noted that productivity is narrowly defined in terms of economic potential. Both ends of the life cycle are viewed as unproductive, children and the aged. The middle-aged are perceived as carrying the burdens imposed by both groups (Butler, 1969). Children, however, are viewed as having future economic potential. In a way, they are seen as an economic investment. Economically, older adults are perceived as a financial liability. This is not to say that older adults are unproductive. However, upon retirement, the older adult is no longer viewed as economically productive in American society and thus devalued.

The fourth factor contributing to ageism in American society and the so-called helping professions is the manner in which aging was originally researched. Poorly controlled gerontological studies have reinforced the negative image of the older adult. When aging was originally studied, researchers went to long-term care institutions where the aged were easy to find. However, only 5% of the older population is institutionalized. Thus, the early research on the aged and aging was based on non-well, institutionalized older individuals. There is still a need for more research to be undertaken using a healthy, community-dwelling older population.

The factors cited above represent four contributing factors to ageism. It has been proposed that individual ageist attitudes can be decreased through continual exposure to and work with older adults (Rosencranz & McNevin, 1969). However, there appears to be a large societal influence on ageist attitudes. Therefore, until these societal influences are addressed, ageism cannot be obliterated. For example, if the fear of death and therefore aging is not somehow addressed in society, then younger individuals will continue to attempt to make the older population somehow different from themselves. This differentiation of themselves from older adults thus serves to protect them from the reality of death.

Few studies have examined the attitudes of older adults toward aging and aged individuals. The majority of these studies have examined the perceptions of older adults using institutionalized aged individuals as subjects. For example, Kastenbaum and Durkee (1964a) surveyed 49 patients who were hospital residents receiving medical, rehabilitative, or psychosocial treatment, and Tuckman and Lavell (1957) used individuals who were residents of a home for the indigent. Hence, sample selection is a major problem for these studies, as institutionalized aged comprise only 5% of the aging population (U.S. Bureau of Census, 1983). Therefore, the negative view of older adults reported in these studies may have been the result of the subjects' own negative experiences of old age and/or life. It should be mentioned here that very little of the empirical research in the field of ageism addresses the cause of ageist attitudes. Rather, it is geared toward the understanding of the ageist attitudes themselves. Woolf (1988) examined the relationship of knowledge of aging with ageist attitudes and found no correlation. In other words, the level of one's ageist attitudes appears to be independent of one's knowledge about aging or the aging process.

The relationship of ageism to self-concept has been the topic of a few studies that examined the impact of ageist attitude on the self-concept of older adults. This is interesting as this represents the group most affected by ageist attitudes. Kastenbaum and Durkee (1964a) discuss how elderly people view old age. They conclude that attitudes of the aged toward themselves as a population is improving. However, it still is hypothesized that as individuals age, their concept of themselves becomes less positive. In support of this contention they cite Kuhlen (1959), who reported that only 5% of older individuals surveyed select middle and later adulthood as the period of greatest happiness. It is important to remember that many of these earlier studies used a nonrepresentative sample of older adults.

One potential outcome of internalized ageist attitudes in the older adult is a syndrome described as the social breakdown syndrome (Kuypers & Bengston, 1973). The social breakdown syndrome is hypothesized to involve seven stages. First, the individual becomes susceptible to dependence on external labeling. This is proposed to occur in response to role loss or the lack of a reference group. For example, retirement or widowhood might make the individual susceptible. The second stage is dependence on external labeling. If this labeling is positive, the syndrome continues no further. However, the third stage is characterized by the societal view of the elderly as incompetent or obsolete. If the individual accepts this negative attitude, he or she falls into assuming a dependent role. This is followed by the atrophy of skills and finally, the labeling of the self as inadequate, incompetent, and "sick." Therefore, what the social breakdown syndrome describes is the self-fulfilling nature of negative attitudes concerning age and aging.

Ageism and its outcomes are similar to those associated with all attempts to discriminate against other groups: persons subjected to prejudice and discrimination tend to adopt the dominant group's negative image and to behave in ways that conform to that negative image (Palmore, 1990, p. 91). Furthermore, the dominant group's negative image typically includes a set of behavioral expectations or prescriptions that define what a person is to do and not to do. For example, the elderly are expected to be asexual, intellectually rigid, unproductive, forgetful, and happy; they are expected to enjoy their retirement and be invisible, passive, and uncomplaining. Ultimately, stereotypes are dehumanizing and promote one-dimensional thinking about others. Elders are not seen as human beings but as objects who, therefore, can be more easily denied opportunities and rights. For example, elders are frequently misdiagnosed or denied medical treatment because they are seen as "old" and, therefore, incurable. Elders are also frequently denied employment or promotion opportunities because they are "old" and less productive. Such discrimination is also evident on the social policy level where the elderly are blamed for having medical problems and consuming public resources rather than seen as having human needs requiring appropriate social responses. Seeing people as objects also increases the likelihood that they may be subjected to abuse and other cruel treatment. Certainly, more research needs to be done in the area of ageism. Unfortunately, the research concerning ageism dropped off precipitously in the 1990s.

4

Older Adults and Urban Neighborhoods

As American society becomes overwhelmed with the number of older adults over the age of sixty-five, there will be a significant number of older adults living in urban neighborhoods; therefore, the design and implementation of age-sensitive housing and elderly-friendly communities will be necessary to promote "aging in place," which allows older adults to live independently for a longer time. To accomplish future urban redevelopment efforts to rebuild downtown areas and urban neighborhoods, American society will no longer be able to ignore the housing preferences and needs of older adults. The combined efforts of meeting the housing preference of older adults in urban neighborhoods, the development of elderly-friendly communities, and the creation of the "Urban Continuum" will retain and attract older adults to live in urban neighborhoods.

The number of Americans between the ages of forty-five and sixty-four has increased by 34% in the past decade. Within the next 25 years there will be over 70 million people over the age of sixty-five. Contemporary urban renewal efforts continue to pull in younger adults and push out older adults. Efforts to relocate an increasing number of older adults into age-segregated housing, such as a continuing-care retirement community, located in a suburban setting perpetuates a false hope that younger adults will be able to sustain the current and future housing market in urban neighborhoods. Clearly stated, over the next 25 years, there will be an increased demand for age-sensitive housing and elderly-friendly neighborhoods from the nearly 70 million older adults over the age of sixty-five.

The success of any senior housing project - whether a continuing-care retirement community built in a rural or suburban setting, or the future development of the "Urban Continuum" model - will be based on the design of housing units that meet the requirements and preferences of older adults who will reside in those housing units.

Over the past several years neighborhood urban redevelopment efforts and some downtown urban redevelopment projects have focused on retail and business sectors to revitalize these areas. Today, urban redevelopment in most major cities incorporates a housing component aimed at attracting young professionals.

Housing research and data indicates that young professionals move more frequently than older adults. In fact, in most cases, older adults prefer not to move in later years. In the city of Cleveland, little has been done to provide housing for older adults in declining neighborhoods and the downtown area. Current urban redevelopment efforts, in neighborhoods such as Tremont, Little Italy, Ohio City, Hough, Edgewater, Saint Clair–Superior, and Cedar-Lee, all have ignored the preferences and needs of the aging population. While the jury is still out on the long-term success of current housing efforts, attracting older adults, as well as young professionals, could have increased the probability of long-term success. Simply stated, there will be more older adults than young professionals living in urban neighborhoods and downtown housing in all major cities in the United States including the city of Cleveland, Ohio, over the next 2 decades.

Current research studies regarding the topic of neighborhood satisfaction and housing preferences for older adults have shed light on questions such as: What are the important factors for creating quality housing for older adults in existing neighborhoods? How do older adults use neighborhood community-based services? Do residents leave their existing neighborhoods due to dissatisfaction with current neighborhood housing options and conditions? Is the growth of the continuing-care retirement community replacing the sense of community often found in urban neighborhoods with a new sense of community? Are perceived ageism attitudes forcing older residents out of existing urban neighborhoods, thus perpetuating age-segregated neighborhoods?

According to the American Association of Retired People (AARP), many older adults are seeking to spend their later years with younger people in urban environments. Gerontologists cite an emerging trend of retirees moving to urban areas, drawn by such factors as public transportation, cultural facilities, and neighbors who are active and young. Based on the information obtained from the American Association of Retired People, the future housing trend of the Multiple-Choice Generation will be a movement back to urban living. Therefore, the traditional ideologies of retirement may no longer make sense.

Current housing options being built in urban neighborhoods as part of local urban redevelopment initiatives in Cleveland, Ohio, present obstacles, challenges, and some difficulties for older adults to remain in their existing homes and neighborhoods and to age in place. For many older adults in Cleveland, Ohio, aging in place in an urban context is challenging.

Today, there is an increased awareness among professionals in the health-care industry that Cleveland's population is aging. This awareness needs to spill over into other professions in order to adequately meet the needs of older adults to age in place. Cleveland's population aging is a product of several factors, such as lower mortality rates, lower fertility rates, and migration patterns. Cleveland's population over the age of sixty-five rose to 9% in 1996 and was expected to increase to 10% in 2001, and it will be over 15% in 2016 (City of Cleveland, 1996).

Since women outlive men by 7 years on average, the population is largely female. Further, 40% of women over the age of seventy-five were living below the low-income cut off (City of Cleveland, 1996). The older residents of Cleveland's neighborhoods are an increasingly diverse group, reflecting the multicultural mosaic of Cleveland's population. In addition, older adults represent an untapped resource, whose participation and contributions can enrich the community.

The growing number of older adults in Cleveland, Ohio, creates opportunities and challenges for the community and various delivery systems to become more responsive to seniors, to create housing options that are age-sensitive, and to become "elderly-friendly."

To promote aging-in-place for older residents in the Saint Hyacinth neighborhood in Cleveland, Ohio, is a challenging undertaking, particularly when taking into account the wide range of services and programs that affect the lives of older adults. These programs and services include transportation, housing, health and mental health care (primary, acute, and long-term care), shopping, safety, leisure, security, outreach, and financial security. Increasing emphasis on community-based programming and community development means that services and resources should be more accessible to seniors where they live.

The future direction of senior housing in Cleveland needs to place an emphasis on housing and the rationale that as the senior population increases, an aging-in-place philosophy must be adopted. This philosophy relates strongly to the concept of "elderly-friendly communities" and "age-sensitive housing." The term *aging-in-place* represents a move from institutional care to community-based care. According to the literature review, older adults prefer to live in their own homes in their own communities whenever possible; however, there are many barriers to achieving this goal.

Despite the Saint Hyacinth residents' repeated preference to stay in their own homes and communities for as long as possible, many residents encounter barriers or obstacles to maintaining an independent lifestyle. These barriers include problems related to physical or emotional health or health services, community-based support services, family and social supports, attitudes about aging, income, housing, mobility and transportation, communication and information, safety and security, and opportunities for activities of one's own choice (National Advisory Council on Aging, May 1989).

Both formal and informal services are needed to help older residents living in urban neighborhoods to remain in their homes. The Western Reserve Area Agency on Aging in Cleveland, Ohio, provides community-based services so that older residents are encouraged to live in their homes and have services delivered to them, which is seen as a positive trend toward quality of life and independence The demand for these services, however, has increased considerably where often the resources available cannot meet the demand.

Successful aging-in-place in elderly-friendly neighborhoods will require that a supportive community offer choices to meet the needs of all residents and also support the ability of people to live independently. A supportive community provides informal and formal supports so that people can age in place and recognizes the diverse needs that people experience as they age, including security, transportation, recreation, shopping, health care, and others.

The purpose of the research case study was to explore whether neighborhood satisfaction is a factor in the decision made by older adults to relocate from their existing home and neighborhood in later years. The research study addressed the following topics: neighborhood satisfaction among older adults, preferred housing options, and the reasons why older adults relocate in later years.

The Saint Hyacinth neighborhood is home to almost 5,000 residents over the age of fifty-five. According to the 2000 U.S. census data, this age cohort represents 24% of the total population of the neighborhood. This age population has decreased by 25% over the past 10 years. The neighborhood has a very successful and active community development organization called Slavic Village Development Corporation.

Over the past 4 years the Slavic Village Development Corporation, process architects, and the deacon of Saint Hyacinth Parish have been working together to determine how to best utilize the vacant school buildings on the church property and the surrounding neighborhood. With an aging resident population, senior housing was a strong consideration as part of the Saint Hyacinth Parish master plan. Up until June 2004, little or no research was conducted on the housing preferences of the older residents in the neighborhood, their level of neighborhood satisfaction, and reasons why residents would move out of their existing home in later years.

The Saint Hyacinth neighborhood in Cleveland, Ohio, was originally part of Newburgh Township; it formed one of the earliest settlements in Cuyahoga County, with New Englanders first arriving in the area in 1796. Newburgh's early growth resulted from its location on high ground, away from the mosquito-infested lowlands of the Cuyahoga River valley, as well as from its proximity to the fast-flowing Mill Creek, which provided the fresh water and power necessary to support development of the area's first industries.

The construction of the Ohio and Erie Canal and the Cleveland and Pittsburgh railroad in the first half of the nineteenth century led to industrial growth and increased commercial trade in the Broadway area, including the establishment of several steel mills. By the mid-1870s, most portions of the original Newburgh Township had been annexed to Cleveland.

The 1870s also brought a large influx of Czech and Polish immigrants to work in the nearby iron and steel mills. The Poles formed their own settlement near Tod Street (today East 65th Street) and Fleet Avenue in the area now known as "Slavic Village." These large residential areas north and south of Fleet Avenue developed after the turn of the century to house the growing Polish population. Fleet and Broadway Avenues, as well as East 65th and East 71st Streets, developed at that time as the main commercial streets in the neighborhood. The neighborhood reached its peak population during the 1920s.

During the 1950s and 1960s, South Broadway experienced substantial out-migration, following the general trend toward suburbanization in Greater Cleveland. As a result, in the 1970s, business activity also decreased, particularly along the secondary retail districts on East 65th and East 71st Streets. Along Broadway, the focus of the retail district shifted from East 55th to Aetna Road, where a modern discount department store and supermarket are now located.

One of the largest housing developments in the city's recent history is the site of the former State of Ohio Developmental Center on Turney Road: "Mill Creek," which is a 200-mixed-unit housing subdivision designed to fit into the existing neighborhood by respecting Cleveland's traditional architecture and acknowledging the surrounding natural environment.

The profile of older adults living in the Saint Hyacinth neighborhood that participated in the study can be summarized as follows: all of the participants were over the age of fifty-five and were industrial working-class individuals with an average median home price of $54,000 and an average median income of $18,000. The educational level of the residents who participated ranged from the completion of the eighth grade to a handful of residents who achieved a 2-year associates degree from a community college. The majority of the participants had a tenth-grade education. The majority of the participants had lived in their current home for at least 40 years and had no intention of moving in the near future.

The variables in this research included age, gender, ethnicity, marital status, living arrangements, and educational level. The 46 participants were members of four separate block clubs, all in the South Broadway neighborhood of Cleveland, Ohio. The block clubs represented in this research are the Saint Hyacinth Block Club, the Fullerton Avenue Block Club, the Fleet Avenue Block Club, and the Union Avenue Block Club. The characteristics of the respondents in all four block clubs are similar.

All of the participants were over the age of fifty-five. Twenty-four participants (52%) were between the ages of fifty-five and sixty-four, 9 participants (20%) were between the ages of sixty-five and seventy-four, and 13 participants (28%) were seventy-five years of age or older.

The 46 participants included 26 females (57%) and 20 males (43%). The ratio of males to females currently living in the Saint Hyacinth neighborhood is fairly even. There are 10,509 males and 10,966 females. However, like in the general older population, there are more older female residents over the age of seventy-five than there are male residents over the age of seventy-five. There are 797 women over the age of seventy-five compared to 403 men over the age of seventy-five. It is noteworthy that there were more single or widowed female participants over the age of seventy-five versus 3 male participants over the age of seventy-five.

The participants included 39 Caucasians (84%) and 7 African-Americans (16%). Over the past 10 years the African-American population in the Saint Hyacinth neighborhood has increased from 322 residents to 4,339 residents. Today, the African-American residents account for 20% of the overall neighborhood population.

Participants in this research included 12 individuals (26%) who were married, 22 individuals (48%) who were divorced or single, and 12 individuals (26%) who were either a widow or a widower. The sample included 31 participants (67%) who lived alone, 11 participants (23%) who lived with a family member, and 4 participants (9%) who lived with a friend or other person. There were more single or widowed women over the age of sixty-five than men who participated in the study. Twenty-one individuals (45%) achieved an eleventh-grade education or less, 14 individuals (30%) achieved a high school diploma, and 11 individuals (23%) completed high school and 2 years of college.

Table 1. Resident Characteristics

	Males	Females	Total
Age 55–64	13	11	24
Age 65–74	4	5	9
Age 75 and older	3	10	13
Caucasian	17	22	39
African-American	3	4	7
Married	6	6	12
Divorced/single	12	10	22
Widowed	2	10	12
Single	12	19	31
Family	7	4	11
Other	1	3	4
Grade 11 or less	15	6	21
High school	7	7	14
2-year college	3	8	11

The housing preferences of the Saint Hyacinth neighborhood residents can be summarized as follows: of 46 respondents, 39 (85%) indicated a preference for the single-family housing option over all other housing options. Nine residents (15%) preferred multifamily housing. Among those preferring the single-family housing option, 20 participants (51%) were between the ages of fifty-five and sixty-four, 6 participants (15%) were between the ages of sixty-five and seventy-four, and 13 participants (33%) were seventy-five years of age or older. Seven participants (15%) selected the multifamily housing option as their housing preference over all other options such as apartments, condominiums, and the continuing-care retirement community.

The predominant housing preference among the residents of the Saint Hyacinth neighborhood was the single-family housing option. Currently, according to the 2000 United States census, there are 9,858 housing units in the neighborhood, of which 5,247 units (53%) are single-family units.

Neighborhood Satisfaction among the Residents of the Saint Hyacinth Neighborhood

The residents were asked a series of eleven closed-ended questions regarding neighborhood satisfaction. The questions addressed three topics: personal residence, community services, and neighborhood appearance.

The neighborhood satisfaction questions were as follows:

- How satisfied are you with the interior of your home?
- How satisfied are you with the exterior of your home?
- How satisfied are you with the overall condition of your home?
- How satisfied are you with other homes in your neighborhood?
- How satisfied are you with streets and roads in your neighborhood?
- How satisfied are you with yards and sidewalks in your neighborhood?
- In your neighborhood, is it easy for you to get around?
- Do you have easy access to goods and services?
- Do you have access to good public transportation?
- In your home, do you feel comfortable?

• In your home, do you feel safe?

The answers of the respondents to these questions indicate a high degree of satisfaction with the various aspects of their living situation. Specific answers to these questions follow:

1. Satisfaction with Interior Condition

Fifteen participants (33%) indicated they were very satisfied with the interior condition of their home, 3 participants (6%) indicated they were satisfied, 22 participants (48%) indicated they were satisfied to some degree, and only 6 participants (13%) indicated they were not satisfied at all with the interior condition of their home.

2. Satisfaction with Exterior Condition

Nine participants (20%) indicated they were very satisfied with the exterior condition of their home, 19 participants (41%) indicated they were satisfied, 10 participants (22%) indicated they were satisfied to some degree, and 8 participants (17%) indicated they were not satisfied at all with the exterior condition of their home.

3. Overall Satisfaction

Eight of the participants (17%) indicated they were very satisfied with the overall condition of their home, 11 of the participants (24%) indicated they were satisfied, 16 of the participants (35%) indicated they were satisfied to some degree, and 11 of the participants (24%) indicated they were not satisfied at all with the overall condition of their home.

4. Satisfaction with Other Homes

Nine participants (20%) indicated they were very satisfied with the condition of other homes in the neighborhood, 12 participants (26%) indicated they were satisfied, 17 participants (37%) indicated they were satisfied to some degree, and 8 participants (17%) indicated they were not satisfied at all with the condition of other homes in the neighborhood.

5. Satisfaction with Streets and Roads

There was less satisfaction indicated in the respondents' answers concerning the condition of the streets and roads. Among the participants, 24 participants (51%) indicated they were satisfied to some degree, and 21 participants (49%) indicated they were not satisfied at all with the condition of the roads and streets in the neighborhood.

6. Satisfaction with Yards and Sidewalks

Nine participants (20%) indicated they were satisfied with the condition of the yards and sidewalks in the neighborhood, 7 participants (15%) indicated they were satisfied to some degree, and 30 participants (65%) indicated they were not satisfied at all with the condition of yards and sidewalks in the neighborhood. This question regarding resident satisfaction with neighborhood yards and sidewalks had the largest percentage of dissatisfied residents. Resident dissatisfaction was represented in all three of the age categories. The 30 participants (65%) who indicated they were not at all satisfied with the condition of the yards and the sidewalks includes 17 participants (35%) between the ages of fifty-five and sixty-four, 4 participants (10%) between the ages of sixty-five and seventy-four, and 9 participants (20%) seventy-five years of age or older.

7. Satisfaction with Mobility

Twenty-four participants (51%) indicated they agreed that getting around the neighborhoods was easy, and 21 participants (49%) indicated they did not agree. These responses indicate an even split in the evaluation of mobility and getting around in the neighborhood.

8. Access to Goods and Services

Twelve participants (26%) indicated they strongly agree that they have easy access to goods and services in their neighborhood. Six participants (13%) indicated they agree, 17 participants (40%) indicated they somewhat agree, and 10 participants (21%) indicated they disagree that they have easy access to goods and services in their neighborhood. The majority of all the participants (76%) agreed that they have easy access to goods and services in their neighborhood.

9. Access to Public Transportation

The majority of all participants (91%) agree that they have access to good and reliable public transportation. Fourteen participants (30%) indicated they strongly agree that they have easy access to good and reliable public transportation in their neighborhood. Six participants (13%) indicated they agree, 22 participants (48%) indicated they somewhat agree, and 4 participants (9%) indicated they disagree with the statement that they have easy access to good and reliable transportation in their neighborhood.

10. Neighborhood Comfort

Fourteen participants (30%) indicated they strongly agree that they feel comfortable in their neighborhood. Fourteen participants (30%) indicated they agree, 6 participants (14%) indicated they somewhat agree, and 12 participants (26%) indicated they disagree with the statement that they feel comfortable in their home and neighborhood. Thirty-four participants (74%) indicated they feel comfortable to some degree in their home in their neighborhood.

11. Neighborhood Safety

Five participants (11%) indicated they strongly agree that they feel safe in their neighborhood, 6 participants (13%) indicated they agree, 20 participants (43%) indicated they somewhat agree, and 15 participants (33%) indicated they disagree with the statement that they feel safe in their neighborhood. Thirty-one participants (67%) indicated they feel safe to some degree in their neighborhood.

Table 2. Satisfaction with Neighborhood

	Very Satisfied	Satisfied	Somewhat Satisfied	Dissatisfied
Interior of home	33%	6%	48%	13%
Exterior of home	20%	41%	22%	17%
Overall	17%	24%	35%	24%
Other houses	20%	26%	37%	17%
Street condition			51%	49%
Yards/sidewalk		20%	15%	65%
Mobility		51%		49%
Goods & services	26%	13%	40%	21%
Transportation	30%	13%	48%	9%
Comfort	30%	30%	14%	26%
Safety	11%	13%	43%	33%

In summary, the majority of the residents between the ages of fifty-five and sixty-four were only somewhat satisfied with the interior, exterior, and overall condition of their home. The majority of the residents aged sixty-five and older were very satisfied with the interior, exterior, and overall condition of their home. This may explain why more residents between the ages of fifty-five and sixty-four had plans to relocate.

Nine of the 24 participants (37%) between the ages of fifty-five and sixty-four had plans to relocate in the future. Only 5 of the 22 participants (22%) aged sixty-five and older had plans to relocate in the future.

Factor Analysis of Neighborhood Satisfaction Questions

Factor analysis was used to determine the internal structure of the neighborhood satisfaction questions. Searching for a structure within the eleven questions relating to neighborhood satisfaction, employing the Rotated Component Matrix procedure, indicated that there are three components comprising satisfaction with the neighborhood. The components are personal residence, community services, and appearance of their neighborhood.

The first component, personal residence, included the questions pertaining to satisfaction with the interior of their home, satisfaction with the exterior condition of their home, the overall satisfaction with their home, and the degree of comfort and safety.

The second component, community services, included the questions pertaining to ease of mobility within the neighborhood, access to goods and services, and public transportation.

The third component, neighborhood appearance, included the questions pertaining to satisfaction with the yards and sidewalks in the neighborhood, satisfaction with the roads and streets in the neighborhood, and the appearance of other houses in the neighborhood.

Table 3. Factor Analysis of Neighborhood Satisfaction: Rotated Component Matrix

	Factor 1	Factor 2	Factor 3
Interior of home	.917	.116	.103
Exterior of home	.908	−.010	.300

Table 3. Factor Analysis of Neighborhood Satisfaction: Rotated Component Matrix (Continued)

	Factor 1	Factor 2	Factor 3
Overall satisfaction	.919	.100	.023
Other houses	−.125	.497	.799
Condition of streets	.347	−.073	.817
Yards/sidewalks	.283	−.089	.857
Mobility	.298	.912	−.077
Goods and services	.201	.911	−.077
Transportation	−.031	.716	.475
Comfort	.901	.204	.142
Safety	.711	.437	.197

Following reliability testing of the questions comprising the neighborhood satisfaction measure, the alpha coefficients ranged from .857 to .880 with a combined alpha coefficient for all eleven questions of .881.

The eleven questions were used to ascertain the difference between those residents who indicated a preference to stay and those who indicated a preference to leave the neighborhood.

Of the personal residence factor questions, the interior of the home (P = .002), the exterior of the home (P = .048), the overall condition of the home (P = .000), and both comfort (P = .001) and safety (P = .014) differentiated significantly between those indicating a preference to stay and those wishing to relocate.

Of the community service factor questions, only transportation (P = .005) differentiated significantly between those indicating a preference to stay and those wishing to relocate.

Of the neighborhood appearance questions, other homes, the condition of yards and sidewalks, and the condition of roads and streets did not differentiate significantly between those indicating a preference to stay and those wishing to relocate.

Responses to Elderly-Friendly Communities by Residents of the Saint Hyacinth Neighborhood

The 46 residents were asked four closed-ended questions that address the topic of elderly-friendly communities.

The residents were asked the following questions:

- Do you feel the housing options in your neighborhood address your needs?

- Do you feel new housing projects are being built to attract older residents?

- Do you feel efforts are being made to ensure that you can remain in your home for as long as possible?

- Do you feel a sense of community within your neighborhood?

The responses indicated that 22 participants (48%) felt there was a sense of community within their neighborhood. Thirty-eight of the participants (83%) felt that the housing options in the neighborhood did not meet their needs and that new projects were being built to attract older adults. Forty participants (86%) felt that no efforts were being made to ensure that older residents in the Saint Hyacinth neighborhood could remain in their existing homes for as long as possible.

Responses to Age-Sensitive Housing by the Residents of the Saint Hyacinth Neighborhood

The 46 participants were asked three closed-ended questions that address the topic of age-sensitive housing.

The residents were asked the following questions:

- Would you move to an age-segregated community?

- Do you believe there is a sense of community in your neighborhood that can be duplicated in a retirement community in the suburbs?

- Do you believe your existing neighborhood is where you want to live no matter how bad the conditions may become over the next several years?

The resident responses indicated that 22 participants (48%) felt there was a sense of community within their neighborhood that could not be duplicated in a retirement community in the suburbs. Thirty-seven of the participants (80%) indicated they would not move to an age-segregated community. Thirty-two participants (70%) believed their existing neighborhood is where they want to live no matter how bad the conditions become over the next several years.

Responses to Plans to Relocate by the Residents of the Saint Hyacinth Neighborhood

The 46 participants were asked if they had plans to relocate in the future. Thirty-two participants (70%) indicated they had no plans to relocate from their existing home in their existing neighborhood in the near future. Fourteen participants (30%) indicated they did have plans to relocate in the near future. The 14 participants included 13 men and 1 woman.

Reasons for Relocation in Later Years

The 46 residents in the sample were asked the question, What would be the number one reason why you would relocate and move out of your existing home and existing neighborhood in later years? The responses were collapsed into the following categories: health reasons, crime, better weather, and the response, "There is no reason why I would move."

Thirty-two participants (70%) indicated there is no reason why they would move out of their existing home. Five participants (10%) indicated they would move out of their existing home for health reasons, 5 participants (10%) indicated they would move out of their existing home because of crime and safety, and 5 participants (10%) indicated they would move for better weather.

The 14 residents (30%) with plans to relocate were asked the following open-ended question: What is the reason why you are planning to move out of your existing home and neighborhood?

The resident responses included the following replies:

Resident 1:	"I am waiting for an opening at the Veterans Hospital in Cleveland."
Resident 2:	"I am hoping to move in with a family member."
Resident 3:	"There is too much work around the place for me to keep up with."
Resident 4:	"My friend, she moved to a senior apartment near her children and I think I would like to move there also, a very clean place, I have been there to visit her."
Resident 5:	"The neighborhood is changing and all my friends are gone."
Resident 6:	"I only moved here for a short time until I can get my life back on track and find a better job - this is all I could really afford after my divorce."
Resident 7:	"My family says I am not really as safe as I used to be in the old neighborhood."
Resident 8:	"I actually planned to move with my wife before we got separated, just a year ago - so I am still thinking about it - maybe."
Resident 9:	"City hall is pushing us out."
Resident 10:	"We are helping our daughter out, watching her six-year-old daughter, and there is no safe place for her to play. I am always worried about her and my daughter in this neighborhood."

Resident 11:	"I have a new job and so I am moving closer to work. I only have a few more years, so being closer will make the next few years easier."
Resident 12:	"Moving into assisted living in Mayfield Heights."
Resident 13:	"After my sister died I did not think I would stay even this long. I'm moving closer to my family."
Resident 14:	"Too much upkeep and work for one person."

The 14 residents (30%) with plans to relocate were asked a series of eight closed-ended questions regarding factors that may have influenced their decision to relocate.

The questions were as follows:

1. Are you relocating to a home that is very similar to your current home?

2. Are you relocating to a suburban neighborhood?

3. Are you relocating to another urban neighborhood?

4. Are you relocating to what you consider to be a nicer neighborhood?

5. Was crime a factor in your decision to relocate?

6. Was neighborhood transportation a factor in your decision to move?

7. Are you relocating to a retirement community?

8. Are the current housing options in your neighborhood a factor in your decision to relocate from your home?

The resident responses indicated that 12 participants (26%) were not moving to a similar home in another urban neighborhood. The same 12 participants (26%) indicated that both crime and the current housing options were factors in their decision to relocate. Thirteen participants (28%) were relocating to what they believed to be a nicer neighborhood. None of the 14 residents who indicated they were moving in the future had plans to relocate to a retirement community.

The residents of the Saint Hyacinth neighborhood in Cleveland, Ohio, exemplify one reason for encouraging older urban residents to remain in their existing homes and their existing neighborhoods. The resident participants overwhelmingly reported that they wanted to grow old in their homes and their existing neighborhood. The resident responses are consistent with other research studies and literature on the topics of relocation in later years and neighborhood satisfaction among older adults.

Elderly-friendly communities and age-sensitive housing that provide the necessary housing options and preferences, community supports, and services that enable older adults to age in place will be the most cost-effective model for aging. Nursing homes not only are an expensive way of delivering services but also tend to propel people who may not require such intense care into the system. The new direction in housing America's seniors will be more health and less health care: keeping older adults active and healthier longer, thus allowing them to age in place in their existing homes in their existing neighborhoods.

5

Aging-in-Place: A New Direction

W hile aging is a natural progression in life, the local city governments and local community development organizations have not braced themselves for one of the fastest-growing populations in the world. In 10 years, nearly 10,000 people will turn sixty-five each day. As millions of older adults who are part of the Multiple-Choice Generation begin to retire, urban neighborhoods will witness a dramatic shift in economic and social forces.

This dramatic shift in economic and social forces among older adults living in urban neighborhoods could be a result of the way in which American society supports aging-in-place and elderly-friendly communities for older adults.

There are three components that influence the decision of older residents living in urban neighborhoods to relocate in later years: personal residence, community services, and neighborhood appearance. These three components are consistent with the philosophy and views of Partners for Livable Communities, a non-profit, Washington, D.C. based organization that views retrofitting existing housing, public transportation, and quality of life crucial to the development of livable and elderly-friendly communities for the rapidly increasing senior population.

A recent report to Congress by the Commission on Affordable Housing and Health Facility Needs for Seniors in the 21st Century has deemed the growing requests of the increasing number of elderly Americans to be a "quiet crisis." While the topic of aging has been a main agenda within the professional aging lobbies, health care, and the elderly population, it has caught the attention of only a few outside organizations.

In August of 1998, Partners for Livable Communities initially focused on design and culture as resources for livability and elderly-friendly communities. Two years later, Partners launched a program to document the economic value of design and cultural amenities. The Economics of Amenity program illustrated how amenities and the quality of life in a community are linked to economic development and job creation. Through conferences like the 1981 Arts Edge Conference in Pittsburgh and publications on various aspects of design and amenity of cities, Partners emerged as a national resource on the economic value of using amenities for community development. Cities were changing, and livability involved more than open spaces and concert halls. It involved managing the social and physical changes that affect every community.

During the early 1990s, Partners continued to broaden its definition of livability. The Shaping Growth in America program added a human dimension that involved social equity, children and families, minorities, and the poor. One of the lessons of Shaping Growth has been that people, jobs, place, leadership, and finance are what make up the agenda for American communities. The 1990s also brought a new name - Partners for Livable Communities - and the redefinition of Partners' Resource Center as the National Center for Community Action. Underlying both is Partners' firm belief that social equity and human potential are the most important elements of a livable community.

As the dynamics of American communities and neighborhoods evolve, organizations that work to make communities and urban neighborhoods more livable and elderly-friendly must also evolve to meet the emerging challenges that face communities in the twenty-first century. Partners' program development and organizational policies were redefined to emphasize broad and equitable citizen participation. Redefining rather than reinventing organizational goals allowed Partners to continue to apply its traditional strength as a civic improvement resource.

In order to promote and create elderly-friendly communities where older adults can age in place, more leadership organizations must work to improve the livability of older urban neighborhoods by promoting quality of life, economic development, and social equity for older adults. Local governments and community development organizations need to work together to set a common vision for the future for the social and physical stability of urban neighborhoods, discover new resources for community and economic development, and build public and private coalitions to further the goal of aging-in-place in urban neighborhoods.

The neighborhood community development organization can promote livable communities and elderly-friendly communities through technical assistance, leadership training, workshops, design charettes, research, and publications. With the assistance from state, national, international, public, private, and media organizations, neighborhood community development organizations can develop a resource network to advocate for older adult residents.

Aging-in-place is a relatively new and complex concept. It is complex in that it involves the aging of both individuals and their homes over time. The premise is that residents' needs are changing but housing and the community remain static.

By the year 2030, 1 in 5, or 80 million Americans, will be termed elderly. The United States will be confronted with unprecedented demands on its already strained social services, appropriate housing issues, and transportation problems. While each urban neighborhood or community cannot be placed in a one-size-fits-all aging model, it is imperative for community and regional cooperation to take the initiative on this rising dilemma.

People are living longer in the United States. Advances in medicine and health care, more in-depth knowledge of healthy lifestyles, and an increase in environmental standards have promoted longevity in humans. The consequences of a prolonged life are multifaceted. The issue of health-care services for the elderly is getting a lot of attention. But as the senior population grows, challenges in urban housing, transportation, and quality of life are also dramatically increasing.

Without a doubt, the senior aging process is filled with many difficulties. Many barriers prevent older persons from remaining a part of their existing neighborhood or community, and not enough emphasis is placed on developing a realistic, workable strategy to overcome the issue of relocating in later years. The process of aging crosses racial, jurisdictional, and socioeconomic boundaries to reach millions of people across the nation. The subject of aging eventually affects everyone, becoming a sizable quality-of-life issue.

The Need for Age-Sensitive Housing

The residents of the Saint Hyacinth neighborhood in Cleveland, Ohio, exemplify one reason for encouraging older urban residents to remain in their existing homes and their existing neighborhoods. The resident participants overwhelmingly reported that they wanted to grow old in their homes and their existing neighborhood. This is consistent with other research and literature on the topic of relocation in later years. Another rationale is that providing the necessary home, community supports, and services that enable older adults to age in place has shown to be the most cost-effective model for aging. Nursing homes not only are an expensive way of delivering services but also tend to propel people who may not require such intense care into the system. The new direction in housing America's seniors will be improved health and less health care: keeping older adults active and healthier longer, thus allowing them to age in place.

Although 89% of older adults claim they want to grow old in their own homes, for many this is not possible. Many American communities cannot support appropriate housing needs for seniors living in their own homes. Ideally, seniors should be able to find housing that best suits their particular situation. But too often, many seniors go straight from their house to a nursing home or assisted-living care facility with few options in between.

In 2001, there were 21 million households headed by older adults aged sixty-five or older. Of these, 80% were homeowners. Older adult property owners face increasing maintenance over the need to make modifications to their homes while their own health and their ability to cope with these issues are deteriorating. Retrofitting homes for safety to accommodate changing health needs and providing medical and fitness programs and other kinds of support systems are practical and effective measures for aging-in-place. Certain home modifications are necessary based on individual health and mobility, no matter where the home is located.

While many increasingly turn to assisted-living facilities to solve the problem, they fail to see a structure of livability that will benefit all groups and strengthen communities on a broad level. This strategy would allow the elderly to live at home longer, significantly increasing the diversity and vitality of a neighborhood, and allow older adults to have more independence.

Neighborhood Transportation

Urban neighborhoods with a high percentage of older adults must take into consideration transportation programs that support a variety of people's needs. While many urban and metropolitan areas have several public transportation options, the majority of public transportation systems are not yet fully integrated or have significant gaps in service and access. Although many seniors still have a driver's license, there will be a time when they are unable to drive themselves and must change their lifestyle to accommodate new developments.

According to the Public Policy Institute Fact Sheet "Transportation: The Older Person's Interest," the elderly use private vehicles more than any other mode of transportation, traveling as a passenger or a driver. Even in urban areas where public transit is more accessible and less expensive, private vehicles are still preferred by the majority of older people. Due to convenience, comfort, and accessibility, it is important for able seniors to drive. Yet by continuing to focus on driving, we are deliberately creating places with the built-in necessity for driving and thereby eliminating options.

Driving is not an option for nearly 7 million older Americans, sixty-five years of age and older. Of these 7 million, individuals are more likely to walk than take public transportation. Using this information, communities must advocate walking and make mass transit more appealing to this demographic. Issues of fear for personal safety, inconvenience, and difficulties in negotiating the system are factors that deter the elderly from using public transportation. Design issues can pertain to the specific needs of the elderly but take the entire community into account as well. More benches at bus stops, additional street lighting, increased signage, and wider sidewalks can be designed for seniors but ultimately benefit all community members, even visitors.

Quality of Urban Life in Later Years

Urban residents with limited discretionary income and time on their hands can contribute more than a friendly presence in the community. Retired older adults have invested significant time and money into communities, making them large economic generators. Elders have given hours through volunteer activities such as mentoring schoolchildren, providing child care, and aiding various public programs. Forty-five percent of people over the age of sixty-five volunteer annually, donating almost 2 billion hours of their time and expertise worth $22 billion. By controlling the majority of wealth in this country, seniors have supported local arts and cultural programs through philanthropic donations, boosted economic development in communities and regions, and donated billions of hours to community service.

Yet older adults can only contribute to economic development if a broad-based community is understood. If seniors cannot use public transportation or walk to the city center to eat lunch and buy a book, or experience a play or lecture, they cannot make as strong an impact. Leaders must see their community through a holistic eye. If mixed housing is not an option, transportation is limited, and seniors are stuck in a nursing home, there is a direct effect on the economic impact the elderly will make.

Public Policy and Aging-in-Place: Identifying the Problems and Potential Solutions

The concept of aging-in-place is relatively new. However, over the past 3 years public policy has made some progress on four key components that both encourage and recognize aging-in-place. The first component is the need for services and a supportive physical environment to help cope with decreased abilities related to chronic conditions such as arthritis, heart disease, or vision problems, which often necessitate a different kind of environment. The second component is the cost of developing new construction. It is sometimes less expensive to support someone in their current residence than to move them to something new or to build something new. The third component is the realization of the expense of housing older persons in nursing homes. The fourth component is the increasing recognition that older persons express a strong preference for aging-in-place and continuity in their living arrangements. For most, housing represents security, proximity to friends and services, and memories of where they raised their families. When older adults consider moving, they indicate very strong preferences for living in residential-type settings; for care facilities, older adults strongly prefer small homes providing care to a fewer number of people.

Age-sensitive housing in urban neighborhoods and elderly-friendly communities will promote aging-in-place, if the following five types of housing solutions are made available to older adult residents living in urban neighborhoods. The options are home modifications, multiple-dwelling units, naturally occurring retirement communities, new housing options, and life cycle communities and universal design.

Home Modifications

There is a classic statement that says, "We shape our houses and afterwards they shape us." Home modifications and adaptations to the physical environment can make it easier and safer to complete the activities of daily living. Design modifications can enhance independence, make it easier for caregivers, improve safety, and reduce accidents.

However, most people are more likely to change their behavior than to change their environment. The barriers to home modification include the cost and the lack of funding mechanisms, a lack of consumer awareness of both the problems and the solutions, lack of linkages between consumers and suppliers, and the stigma of "institutional" features such as grab bars.

Multiple-Dwelling Units

Existing multiple-dwelling units, such as apartment complexes, are a valuable and irreplaceable supply of housing for seniors. These are a very successful form of affordable housing, one which was intended for independent older persons. However, as residents have aged, the need for assistance has increased.

The solution is to provide physical design modifications and supports to facilitate aging-in-place. In California, a pilot program has provided such buildings with housing coordinators who link residents to existing community services and supports and who identify and develop additional supports that are needed. This has proven to be an effective, economical strategy for supporting older persons in their own homes.

Naturally Occurring Retirement Communities

Naturally occurring retirement communities are areas or buildings populated by large concentrations of the elderly. A 1992 survey found that 27% of the older adults lived in a building or neighborhood where more than 50% of older residents were over the age of sixty. These places are termed naturally occurring retirement communities because they were not intentionally planned for older persons.

The problem with naturally occurring retirement communities is that they lack the amenities, services, housing, and infrastructure to adequately support aging-in-place. Some of these places are neighborhoods in which a cohort of once younger persons has aged in place. Other settings include small rural towns where there has been out-migration of younger persons. Naturally occurring retirement communities offer the potential for economies of scale - these areas represent ideal places to cluster services, locate services, and provide transit and zoning for a range of housing types.

New Housing Options

New housing options include accessory apartments, granny flats or garden homes, assisted-living facilities, and small group settings with shared care. The need is for a range of housing to respond to different preferences and situations of older persons. Such residential housing options are key for persons who need more supervision, support, and services than can easily be provided in their own home. There is especially a pent-up demand for service-enriched housing that emphasizes privacy, autonomy, and choice.

Life Cycle Communities and Universal Design

Many of the physical problems that existing housing and neighborhoods present for older persons would be eliminated if we intentionally planned supportive and flexible communities. A worldwide movement is emerging advocating adaptable housing and age-sensitive communities. Universal design and life cycle housing encourages mixed use of housing, higher densities in certain areas, pedestrian-oriented communities, new forms of transportation, new forms of housing, and new forms of technology.

However, housing alone will not permit older adults, primarily single women or widowed women over the age of sixty-five, to age in place and live their later years in their existing homes. The predicted future for urban residents to age in place will be to integrate the services of a continuing-care retirement community into the neighborhood, creating the "Urban Continuum." The "Urban Continuum" will evolve similar to the manner in which free stand-alone hospitals can no longer compete in the medical arena. An independent, or stand-alone, continuing-care retirement community will not be able to compete with the larger retirement community conglomerations. Due to the increased cost of operations and the increased cost of providing goods and services, retirement communities will be consolidated. The integration of services to residents living in nearby neighborhoods will increase the longevity of the continuing-care retirement community. The outreach of home service to residents living in urban areas who want to stay in their existing homes will include assistance with daily activities, health and wellness programs, and quality-of-life issues.

6

Elderly-Friendly Communities and the "Urban Continuum"

The Elderly-Friendly Community Doctrine was developed to promote aging-in-place for older adults living in urban neighborhoods and to allow for future generations of older adults to age in place and stay in their existing homes in later years.

The first objective of the doctrine is to acknowledge the diversity among older adult in urban neighborhoods. Existing housing and support models have not creatively responded to a population that is becoming more culturally diverse. Ethnic diversity will be increasingly important in the future, bringing with it among some groups a greater preference for caring for the family and aging relatives. Policy needs to promote housing models that are sensitive to ethnic and cultural preferences for extended family living.

The second objective of the doctrine is to treat older adults as consumers. As consumers, older adults can provide information and can create demand. Equally, as consumers they need to receive information on options and choices that affect quality-of-life issues, such as housing.

The third objective of the doctrine is to shift the paradigm of senior housing from the nursing home setting to appropriate housing options and community-based services. Older adults who are cognitively or physically impaired but not in need of intensive nursing services can live in a variety of settings with supportive physical features and linkages to services often at less cost to the government.

In a recent study conducted by the School of Medicine at the University of California in Los Angeles, one-third of very chronically ill older adults indicated they would rather die than move to a nursing home. Older adults, families, and professionals agree that the nursing home, with its lack of privacy and highly structured medical environment, should primarily serve rehabilitation and transitional needs rather than long-term residential care needs. There is a clear need to develop a range of housing options with supportive physical features and service linkages.

The fourth objective of the doctrine is to overcome domain problems among organizations. Aging-in-place requires coordination of policies and priorities from a number of sources and agencies at the federal, state, and local level.

The fifth objective of the doctrine is to devise comprehensive approaches. The preferences and resources of older adults and their families vary considerably among the Multiple-Choice Generation, the Limited-Choice Generation, and the No-Choice Generation, as do the needs of particular communities. One size does not fit all, and a range of housing types should be provided.

The sixth and final objective of the doctrine is to create new models of housing that facilitate age-integration and age-sensitive design and that are colocated with community amenities. The overall goal of the doctrine is to "insulate, not isolate."

The Elderly-Friendly Community Doctrine is rooted in the belief that aging-in-place is not just about housing or programs but rather about the value that society places on older adults themselves.

Strategies to Create Elderly-Friendly Communities

Aging-in-place involves more than the ability to stay in one's home. It means being able to stay in one's neighborhood and to continue to participate as a member of the community. Many seniors experience increasing isolation as walking becomes more difficult or driving is no longer possible. Therefore, community features such as public transportation or shops within short walking distances, well-lit, flat, and even walking routes, and other community amenities are all important features of an integrated community that supports aging-in-place.

The "Relevant System" developed by Dr. Raaijmakers measures these types of community attributes and has the capacity to evaluate and analyze the relationships among numerous different environmental elements. His research explores the metaphorical concept of "residential friendly zones for the elderly." His methodology can be used to evaluate the suitability of existing areas and can also be used as a tool for policy and planning.

In addition to mapping land use and environmental characteristics, the research method also includes extensive surveys with local seniors and service providers, including those involved in the housing industry. A parallel concept, that of "residential preference areas," allows the synthesis and overlaying of subjective information about the neighborhoods with the objective, physical, and social data. These layers of information can be graphically mapped and represented in public meetings and planning sessions. An ongoing dialogue involving all the local stakeholders, most importantly the seniors themselves, is aimed at developing a policy document. Plans are made for changes in the local area to support and enhance residential areas where seniors prefer to live and where independent aging can be best supported.

Research projects in various neighborhoods of Amsterdam and Utrecht in the Netherlands have allowed the continual refinement of the GIS system and participatory planning methods. Results of the planning process to date have been encouraging, and many important policy and program changes have taken place in the subject neighborhoods as a result of the research, as well as new housing projects being planned. This research tool and its associated methodology are applicable to any setting; the Gerontology Research Centre is currently investigating its use locally for senior housing research. Given the increasing extent to which seniors are choosing to, and having to, age in housing in the community, research such as this significantly contributes to guiding the complex process of evaluating and managing our residential environments and health and support service sectors.

Age-sensitive housing lies within the continuum with accommodation options for seniors between independent living at one end and facility care at the other.

Independent living refers to self-contained single-family housing, town houses, or apartments, which seniors either own or rent and where they function as members of the wider community. In the case of the "Urban Continuum," they also function as part of a retirement community and retirement lifestyle not offered in urban settings. Under the traditional model, if residents do receive any formal care and support, such as home-maker services, home nursing, or meals, the resident or a family member makes this decision and organizes the support.

Facility care means living in a room, not a self-contained dwelling, and eating three meals a day communally. Typically, bathrooms are shared and doors to residents' rooms cannot be locked. Facility care includes a full package of services, including nursing, housekeeping, laundry, and meal service, and this package is rarely negotiable. Facility residents are generally not considered, or treated as, members of the wider community.

Catered living fills the gap between these two options. It is not nursing care, nor is it completely independent living. It is in-between. It meets the needs of seniors who may want some help with their everyday lives, or even just some security, 24 hours a day, 7 days a week, but who do not need regular nursing care.

The emphasis in "catered living" and "age-sensitive housing" is on residents' independence, balanced with their need for round-the-clock security, daily assistance with everyday chores, such as shopping and maintenance, and opportunities for social interaction with peers.

The essence of age-sensitive housing has been expressed many times by seniors who say, "I've got privacy, but I know help is there if I need it!"

Age-sensitive housing, in its narrowest definition, refers to secure, congregate housing where seniors live in private, self-contained suites and one or two meals a day are served in a communal dining room.

Age-sensitive housing, in the broadest sense, includes an array of housing with support options for seniors. The essential features are independence with security and help with everyday tasks when needed.

The Need for Age-Sensitive Housing

The need for age-sensitive housing for seniors in urban neighborhoods is growing for three major reasons: (1) there are fewer facility beds available to older people than in the past when facility placement was a foregone conclusion for elderly people; (2) access to home support services has become more restrictive due to fiscal restraints; and (3) the older population has made it clear that they prefer housing that offers independence with support.

Seniors' first preference is to remain in their own homes as long as they can manage on their own or with community support services. When maintenance and shopping become overwhelming, however, and social isolation results from lack of mobility, lack of money, and a dwindling number of friends, then a move to supportive housing is considered.

As stated earlier, in reference to the residents of the Saint Hyacinth neighborhood, older adults wish to remain in their own neighborhood or a community nearby if they move from their home to a more supportive environment. Staying in the same community lessens the trauma of relocation, increases the chances of remaining part of their established social network, and allows them to continue with the same doctor, pharmacist, and so on.

The need for supportive housing for seniors is under demographic pressures in other parts of the world as well. The number of seniors living in Canada will balloon as Canada's 10 million baby boomers reach their later years; the first wave of boomers turned fifty this year. By 2020, seniors aged sixty-five and older will comprise 17% of the Canadian population.

The option of living in the same household as their adult children and grandchildren is not as popular among American seniors; only approximately 3% do so. This option is not viable for most families, given the increasing labor force participation of women, who are the primary caregivers of the elderly, and the notable mobility of Americans.

Models and Approaches to Age-Sensitive Housing

There are numerous ways that Catered Living can be provided to seniors in America. Seniors can stay in their own house, move to an independent unit near their children, or move to housing specially designed for older people where they can be near others their own age. Some of these options provide more support than others; some are more expensive than others. Following are ten alternative models or approaches to providing supportive living for seniors to remain in their own home for as long as possible.

1. **Home sharing** - This is an arrangement by which a senior opens his or her home to another person wishing to share the accommodation and provide support and companionship. The home provider and home sharer are matched by a community agency. Home sharing has the advantages of using existing housing stock, providing affordable rental accommodation, and offering security to old people who live alone. The support provided by the renter can be minimal or more. This housing option supplements a senior's income. Home sharing has been a housing option for seniors in Canada for about 20 years, but reductions in funding for social agencies to coordinate it has reduced the number of matches that can be made.

2. **In-home suites** - Similar in nature to guest quarters or a studio built into or onto existing housing stock, in-home suites (referred to in the United States as "in-law suites") can serve the needs of seniors who wish to live close to, but not with, their adult children. An accessory in-home suite has the advantages of both privacy and security. These suites can be illegal, although municipalities often turn a blind eye, knowing that they serve a valuable purpose. Typically, there is a two-way exchange of assistance, until the elderly parent becomes frail or cognitively impaired, at which point support from children exceeds support to children. The cost of this option varies widely, depending on how extensive the renovations are, how large the unit is, and so on.

3. **Garden suites or granny flats** - An Australian concept, "granny flats" are small manufactured houses, usually smaller than 70 square meters, with one bedroom, which are placed on the prop-

erty of a "host house," whose water and electricity supply they tap into. Like accessory apartments, they support independence with security. They are most suitable for the large residential lots found in rural areas and small towns or villages. Granny flats are intended, as the name implies, to house the elderly relative(s) of the occupants of the host house. Granny flats were introduced more than a decade ago in Canada, but they are not widely used due to zoning impediments and decreased government housing subsidies for families or seniors who cannot afford to purchase one.

4. **Age-sensitive housing designed for older adults** - In congregate housing, seniors live in private, secure, self-contained suites in a supervised building or buildings. One or two meals a day are served in a communal dining room. Housekeeping services and social activities are available, if desired. Although emergency assistance is available on-site, medical assistance is not available. Residents of supportive housing have locked doors and a choice of which support services to accept. (A recent survey found that the three most important services to seniors in supportive housing are emergency help, 24-hour security, and weekly cleaning, in that order, for both women and men.) Residents usually function as members of two communities: the small community of their own housing complex, and the wider community. Privately developed supportive housing tends to be "high-end," with costs varying by region.

5. **Abbeyfield houses** - Originating in Great Britain, Abbeyfield houses are typically renovated larger houses in residential neighborhoods. Seven to ten older people live under one roof, under the care of a housekeeper, who prepares meals and does the household shopping. Residents have separate rooms, with lockable doors, and usually have their own bathrooms. They eat together in a traditional dining room. The main aim of Abbeyfield houses is to be homelike, small-scale, supportive, and affordable accommodation for elderly people who are at risk of social isolation and

its related hazards. Abbeyfield houses are very popular in British Columbia and Ontario. They have a difficult time, however, finding adequate funding, especially for the purchase of properties. This group home housing option, which is nonprofit, tends to be more modestly priced than privately developed congregate care. The cost to residents is influenced by the price of land, housing, and renovations.

6. **The age-integrated campus model** - The "campus model" usually refers to clustering independent apartments for seniors, congregate supportive housing for seniors, and nursing home care, all on one site, so that a continuum of care can be provided to residents. Tenure in the apartments and supportive housing may be rental, life lease, or condominium ownership. The advantages of the campus model are as follows: (1) there is no need for more than one commercial kitchen to produce meals for residents of both the nursing home and the supportive housing; (2) staff at the nursing home can provide emergency response to residents of the congregate supportive housing (which will typically have emergency call buttons located in the bathrooms and bedrooms); (3) spouses at different levels of care can be no more than a few minutes' walk apart; (4) capable residents can provide volunteer services to the nursing home; and (5) residents become familiar with the staff and environment of higher levels of care, which may reduce the trauma of moving to a facility. This model exists in a number of locations throughout the United States. In many cases, the nursing home had been in place for some years when the housing was added on the same land. Since high-density zoning was already in place for the nursing home, rezoning for housing was not an issue. The cost of supportive housing in this situation depends on whether or not the land has already been paid for (when the nursing home was built) and other factors, such as location. While the concept of a continuing-care community is favorable for aging-in-place, the model is affordable only to the top 2%

of older adults living in the United States. The model is very expensive.

7. **Renovations and creative conversions** - Existing buildings can become supportive housing through renovation or conversion. Across Canada, the private for-profit sector and the private non-profit sector, including church groups, are renovating and converting existing buildings to provide housing for seniors. In most cases, renovated or converted housing stock provides modestly priced housing for seniors.

8. **Cooperative housing** - Housing cooperatives, whether for seniors only or for families, offer the kind of security and sense of community that many seniors seek. Co-ops are usually in cities. The housing form is typically town houses or apartments. A recent national study of seniors living in age-mixed co-ops showed an almost universal appreciation for the co-op lifestyle and the community support it offers. In general, co-ops are doing a good job as far as older members are concerned. Housing co-ops are usually modest in cost. The support that members provide each other can be quite extensive. Fewer cooperative housing complexes were developed in the 1990s than 20 years ago due to lack of financial assistance from governments.

9. **Modular homes** - Modular homes are becoming more popular as an option that has a strong potential to create cost-effective supportive living environments for older adults, because the housing units are clustered in fairly close proximity, which increases security and social interaction. Manufactured home communities typically have communal space such as a clubhouse, and they tend to attract people of similar background and lifestyle.

10. **Seasonal housing** - During the winter months, typically November through April, in summer tourist destinations across the United States, especially the Southeastern states, motels and hotels offer special monthly rates to seniors. Suites are fully furnished, laundry and housekeeping services are provided, meal plans are

included, and, in some cases, special activity staff are employed. This seasonal supportive housing option for seniors is a win-win situation: it ameliorates the "summer boom, winter bust" cycle of the hospitality industry, and it allows seniors to avoid the risks and isolation of a harsh winter in their rural homes, without giving up their homes.

11. **The restrictions of elderly-friendly communities** - Zoning restrictions are one of the main challenges identified by both private and non-profit developers of elderly-friendly communities and age-sensitive housing options for older adults in urban neighborhoods. Most residential areas, where many of the housing options described above will be located, are zoned for single-family dwellings only. Many municipalities do not seem to have the ability or will to change single-family dwelling zoning to higher densities to accommodate seniors' housing.

Governmental compartmentalization is another restriction that results from the division between health and housing mandates at federal, state, and municipal levels. Housing projects for seniors are not supposed to provide supervision or care to residents, although, in practice, some dedicated housing providers do so, without adequate funding. Other housing providers contend that they "are in the housing business, not the care business" and they, and their well tenants, do not want their buildings to become long-term care facilities.

Lack of Knowledge about Aging

Lack of knowledge about aging is a related challenge in that public housing providers lack education about aging and in particular about cognitive impairment, and those who are interested in providing more supportive living environments need this information to make appropriate physical and staffing changes, which could be done without enormous expenditures.

Lack of Information about Seniors' Housing Needs

There is also a dearth of practical guidelines for families, private developers, and non-profit groups wanting to build supportive housing from scratch. They need information on the following:

- Architectural design for older adults for aging-in-place in urban areas

- The social and psychological needs of older adults in urban areas

- Knowledge of the cultural differences among seniors in urban neighborhoods

- What government assistance, if any, is available to encourage and facilitate development of senior housing in urban areas

- How to prepare for "aging-in-place" of residents in terms of policy, staffing or programming, and architectural design and detailing

Lack of Awareness of the Consequences of Aging-in-Place

Another problem is that many public and private developers of housing for seniors do not seem to recognize that residents will age in place, that is, they will get a year older every year, and with this inevitable aging, their characteristics and needs will change. Housing for seniors is often not flexible enough to allow for these changes. Instead, it is assumed that the occupants must be flexible - that is, they must move elsewhere when they no longer "fit" their housing.

One of the critical issues related to aging-in-place results from the increased prevalence of dementia correlated to age. As the average age of a resident population increases, so does the likelihood of having residents who are cognitively impaired and who may become a risk to themselves or other residents. This situation has been experienced and grappled with in municipal housing, co-op housing, and private-sector housing. Policies and occupancy agreements that address this issue - for example, "exit agreements" stating that the occupant will have to leave if he or she becomes a safety threat to self or neighbors - are being addressed across the country.

Managing Senior Housing Options

Providers of social housing for seniors have started to hire building managers for their ability to communicate and willingness to work with older people, more than for their ability to work on a building. It is understood that technical skills can be learned or the technical work subcontracted, whereas the attitude of the building manager can set the mood for the entire housing complex.

Having the Respect of the Community

Private for-profit and not-for-profit developers of housing for seniors who are familiar with their community get more support from bankers and more response from senior renters or purchasers than out-of-town developers.

Being Flexible about Support

In several supportive housing projects across the United States, much of the support is provided on an informal basis by residents to each other and most of the social activities are planned and carried out by the residents. Some housing providers consciously "let it happen" and then encourage and facilitate whatever develops naturally, rather than impose pre-determined supportive programming.

The "Urban Continuum" is a new direction in aging-in-place in urban neighborhoods. The "Urban Continuum" is a lifetime plan for a lifetime at home. The model is based on the integration of services provided by continuing-care retirement communities to residents living in urban neighborhoods. The preference to stay at home and age in place should be available to all older adults. The retirement lifestyle of the continuing-care retirement community should be a choice available to all older adults. Today only the top 2% of older adults over the age of sixty-five can afford to live in a retirement community that offers a continuum of care. The "Urban Continuum" will make this retirement lifestyle choice available to all.

The Kendal Corporation, headquartered in Kennett Square, Pennsylvania, is a nonprofit organization and a provider of services for older adults.

The Kendal Corporation has launched a new program that incorporates the foundations of the "Urban Continuum." Their program is called *Kendal at Home*. This new, affordable program of continuing-care services gives residents security and peace of mind at all stages of their lives and at all levels of care. And, most importantly, it does so in their existing home in their existing neighborhood.

As participants in the *Kendal at Home* program, residents benefit from a continuing-care agreement to provide this continuum of care in the residents' own home. Should the residents' care needs change unexpectedly, the program options offered would cover routine assistance with daily tasks and also the cost of assisted living and even skilled care in the residents' home or, if required, in a highly qualified area facility.

Participants in the *Kendal at Home* program have a personal care coordinator who takes the burden of resident care off family and friends. Most family members have good intentions and want to help, but the reality of caring for someone as he or she ages can be very demanding and difficult. Residents can turn to their personal care coordinator for guidance and help in finding the care that they need. Family members are involved in decision making if residents want them to be, but they don't have to be responsible for making the decisions alone, searching for quality providers of care, managing the care, and making sure residents are safe.

The "Urban Continuum" model is designed to provide participants with the same types of services offered to residents in a continuing-care retirement community setting. Residents are eligible for services if they have one deficiency in any activities of daily living. These activities include eating, dressing, grooming, transferring, toileting, bathing, walking, and mobility. Services offered to residents living in urban neighborhoods would include the following:

- **Adult day care** - Adult day care programs located throughout the community provide services in a congregate setting for a scheduled number of hours per week, including transportation, meals, and activities.

- **Care coordinator** - Residents will be assigned a personal care coordinator to coordinate any services they may need. The personal care coordinator will work closely with them, their family, and their physician to have the right services delivered to them in their home or, when necessary, in a Kendal-approved facility. A member of the care coordination staff will be available to residents 24 hours a day, 7 days a week.

- **Certified home health aide** - If assistance is needed with personal care, such as bathing or dressing, a licensed home health aide will be provided for residents in their home.

- **Companion/homemaker services** - A companion or homemaker will be provided when assistance is needed with day-to-day chore activities in the resident's home such as cooking, dishwashing, laundry, light housekeeping, and errands. Also, if needed, someone will be available for supervision of, and assistance with, activities of daily living and medication reminders.

- **Emergency response system** - Residents will be provided with an emergency response system with 24-hour coverage when needed.

- **Home inspection** - During the first year of membership and every second year thereafter, residents will have a safety and functional inspection of their home, completed by a licensed occupational therapist, to ascertain any problems and to make recommendations based on the inspection.

- **Home nursing care** - When needed, residents can receive home health-care services provided by a registered nurse or a licensed practical nurse.

- **Meals** - Lunch and dinner can be delivered to residents' homes under certain qualifying conditions for a limited amount of time when they are unable to cook.

- **Nursing home** - If the residents' health changes and they can no longer remain in their home or in residential care or assisted living, nursing home care will be provided.

- **Referral services** - Residents can obtain a referral from the program for any type of service they may need to stay in their home. Exam-

ples of these services are legal, financial planning, home maintenance, and rental of medical equipment.

- **Social and wellness programs** - Social networking, educational
  opportunities, and wellness seminars are offered to residents.

- **Transportation** - Residents will have transportation to and from medi-
  cally necessary outpatient surgery, short procedures, or hospitalization.

The Model History began in 2000, when Kendal at Oberlin began the
process of preparing to offer a continuum-of-care contract for persons
residing in their homes. A legal review was done with Baker & Hostetler,
of Cleveland, Ohio, who verified that there are no Ohio laws to prevent
this type of program from being offered by an existing continuing-care
retirement community. This development is a more natural extension of
Kendal at Oberlin's mission to serve older adults.

In 2001, Kendal at Oberlin received a grant of $50,000 from the Cleve-
land Foundation for the planning phase of the program outlined above
called Kendal at Home. In January and June of 2002 Kendal at Oberlin
received the first and second installment, respectively, of $25,000 each,
toward the Continuing Care at Home project. Kendal at Oberlin utilized
the entire amount of the grant ($50,000) provided by the Cleveland Foun-
dation to complete the planning phase of Kendal at Home.

In 2002, Kendal engaged Cadbury Consulting and Cadbury Continuing Care at Home to assist with the determination of the market and actu-
arial viability of the program. Third Age, Inc., was retained by Cadbury to
conduct the necessary market research.

The research consisted of two phases:

- **Phase I** - Statistical or secondary market research, which included
  conducting key informant interviews, analyzing the demographic
  profile of the potential service areas, and the application of market
  share tests

- **Phase II** - Primary market research consisting of a telephone survey
  and subsequent focus groups

The Cleveland Foundation also awarded Kendal at Home an additional amount of $170,000 to support further development and implementation of the Continuing Care at Home program for Cuyahoga and Lorain Counties. In addition to the Cleveland Foundation, numerous Kendal communities aided this program. Kendal Corporation, Kendal at Hanover, Kendal-Crosslands, and Kendal at Oberlin all provided loans to Kendal at Home. All of these organizations helped to support the launching of this program.

The Kendal at Home program provides a broad range of services and support in members' homes with the goal of keeping them living independently in their community for as long as possible. Similar to the services provided by a continuing-care retirement community but without the campus or facility structure, the Kendal at Home program offers care coordination and commitment to provide needed services, in the home.

In conclusion, American society will soon be overwhelmed with the number of older adults over the age of sixty-five. The question is Where will they live? The answer is that many will live in neighborhoods in all of America's urban cities either by choice or by default. Our American society has a long history of assisting older people in the form of Social Security, meals for shut-ins, and medical insurance. However, Americans have fallen short in one arena that has a profound impact on the quality of day-to-day living - housing.

Housing that is well designed, suitably located, and affordable contributes to the ability of an older person to maintain his or her independence and to age in place. The current housing options available in urban neighborhoods are limited and are becoming a crucial factor in determining the physical, social, and emotional well-being of older adults.

The current and future need for appropriate age-sensitive housing in elderly-friendly communities in urban neighborhoods will be dictated by the demands made by seniors to remain in their existing homes for as long as possible and to age in place. The movement toward creating elderly-friendly communities in America's urban neighborhoods will be dictated by the desire of older Americans to live independently, by the lack of long-term care facilities, and by demographic pressures.

Private for-profit and non-profit developers, as well as public housing providers, need information, education, encouragement, and assistance so that they can create and manage supportive housing that is flexible enough to accommodate aging-in-place.

Glossary of Terms

Accreditation:

A seal of approval given by an autonomous governing body to a community or service provider. To become accredited, the community or provider must meet specific requirements set by the accreditation entity and is then generally required to undergo a thorough review process by a team of evaluators to ensure certain standards of quality. The accrediting organizations are independent, not government agencies or regulatory bodies. Some examples of accreditation bodies for the senior housing and care industry include CARF (Commission on Accreditation of Rehabilitation Facilities), CCAC (Continuing Care Accreditation Commission), and JCAHO (Joint Commission on Accreditation of Healthcare Organizations).

Activities of Daily Living (ADLs):

Bathing, eating, grooming, dressing, toileting, and other day-to-day activities.

ADA (Americans with Disabilities Act):

Passed by Congress in 1980, this law establishes a clear and comprehensive prohibition of discrimination on the basis of disability.

Administrator:

In most cases, a licensed professional who undertakes the duty of managing the day-to-day operations of a care facility such as a nursing home or an assisted-living facility.

Adult Day Care:

Structured programs with stimulating social activities and health-related and rehabilitation services for the elderly who are physically or emotionally disabled and need a protective environment. The participant is usually brought to the care facility in the morning and leaves in the evening.

Aging-in-Place:

A concept that advocates allowing a resident to choose to remain in his/her living environment regardless of the physical and/or mental decline that may occur with the aging process.

Alzheimer's Care Center:

A treatment center that specializes in providing care for those with Alzheimer's disease with more of the care geared toward supervision of the patient in a safe and controlled environment.

Alzheimer's:

A progressive neurodegenerative disease characterized by loss of function and death of nerve cells in several areas of the brain, leading to loss of mental functions such as memory and learning. Alzheimer's disease is the most common cause of dementia.

Ambulatory:

Able to walk freely and independently; not bedridden or hospitalized.

Assessment:

An evaluation, usually performed by a physician, of a person's mental, emotional, and social capabilities (from AA).

Assisted Living:

A special combination of housing, personalized supportive services, and health care designed to meet the needs - both scheduled and unscheduled - of those who need help with activities of daily living. Services provided in assisted-living residences usually include the following:

- Three meals a day served in a common dining area
- Housekeeping services

- Transportation
- Assistance with eating, bathing, dressing, toileting, and walking
- Access to health and medical services
- 24-hour security and staff availability
- Emergency call systems for each resident's unit
- Health promotion and exercise programs
- Medication management
- Personal laundry services
- Social and recreational activities (from ALFA)

Caregiver:

The primary person in charge of caring for an individual with Alzheimer's disease, usually a family member or a designated health-care professional.

Charge Nurse:

An RN or LPN who is responsible for the supervision of a unit within a nursing facility. The charge nurse schedules and supervises the nursing staff and provides care to facility residents.

Congregate Housing:

Similar to independent living except that it usually provides convenience or supportive services like meals, housekeeping, and transportation in addition to rental housing (from ALFA).

Continuing-Care Retirement Community (CCRC):

A continuing-care retirement community is a community that offers several levels of assistance, including independent living, assisted living, and nursing home care. It is different from other housing and care facilities for seniors because it usually provides a written agreement or long-term contract between the resident (frequently lasting the term of the resident's lifetime) and the community which offers a continuum of housing, services, and health-care system, commonly all on one campus or site (from ALFA).

Continuum of Care:

Care services available to assist individuals throughout the course of a disease. This may include independent living, assisted living, nursing care, home health, home care, and home- and community-based services.

Dementia:

The loss of intellectual functions (such as thinking, remembering, and reasoning) of sufficient severity to interfere with a person's daily functioning. Dementia is not a disease itself but rather a group of symptoms that may accompany certain diseases or conditions. Symptoms may also include changes in personality, mood, and behavior. Dementia is irreversible when caused by disease or injury but may be reversible when caused by drugs, alcohol, hormone or vitamin imbalances, or depression.

Developmental Disability (DD):

Affliction characterized by chronic physical and mental disabilities, which may include cerebral palsy, retardation, thyroid problems, seizures, and quadriplegia.

Director of Nursing (DON):

A DON oversees all nursing staff in a nursing home and is responsible for formulating nursing policies and monitoring the quality of care delivered, as well as the facility's compliance with federal and state regulations pertaining to nursing care.

Financial Counseling Programs:

Programs that help seniors with managing their finances and bills and with completing Medicaid, Medicare, or insurance forms.

HIPAA (The Health Insurance Portability and Accountability Act of 1996):

This act became a law on January 1, 1997. The act states the requirements that a long-term care policy must follow in order that the premiums paid may be deducted as medical expenses and benefits not paid be considered as taxable income.

HMO:

A health maintenance organization (HMO) is an organized system for providing comprehensive health care in a specific geographic area to a voluntarily enrolled group of members.

Home Health Care:

Provision of medical and nursing services in the individual's home by a licensed provider.

Hospice Care:

Philosophy and approach to providing comfort and care at life's end rather than heroic lifesaving measures (from AA); it can include medical, counseling, and social services. Most hospice care is furnished in-home, while specialized hospices or hospitals also provide this service.

Independent Living:

A residential living setting for elderly or senior adults that may or may not provide hospitality or supportive services. Under this living arrangement, the senior adult leads an independent lifestyle that requires minimal or no extra assistance. Generally referred to as elderly housing in the government-subsidized environment, independent living also includes rental-assisted or market-rate apartments or cottages where residents usually have complete choice in whether to participate in a facility's services or programs.

Instrumental Activities of Daily Living (IADLs):

Secondary level of activities (different from ADLs, such as eating, dressing, and bathing) important to daily living, such as cooking, writing, and driving.

Kitchenette:

Each facility may have its own definition of a kitchenette, but generally one includes a sink, cabinet space, a mini-refrigerator, and possibly a microwave. In contrast, a full kitchen would usually have a burner unit, sink, cabinets, a full-size refrigerator, and possibly a microwave or stove.

Licensed Practical Nurse (LPN):

LPNs are trained to administer technical nursing procedures as well as provide a range of health-care services, such as administration of medication and changing of dressings. One year of post-high-school education and passage of a state licensing exam is required.

Life Care Community:

A continuing-care retirement community (CCRC) that offers an insurance-type contract and provides all levels of care. It often includes payment for acute care and physicians' visits. Little or no change is made in the monthly fee, regardless of the level of medical care required by the resident, except for cost-of-living increases.

Long-Term Care:

Care given in the form of medical and support services to persons who have lost some or all of their capacity to function due to an illness or disability.

Long-Term Care Insurance:

The insurance that pays for a succession of caregiving services for the elderly or chronically ill. This care may be provided in a facility (nursing home, mental hospital, etc.) or in the individual's home with a nurse or aide (from LTC Insurance).

Managed Care:

Can best be described as the partnership of insurance and a health-care delivery system. The basic goal of managed care is to coordinate all health-care services received to maximize benefits and minimize costs. Managed care plans use their own network of health-care providers and a system of prior approval from a primary care doctor in order to achieve this goal. Providers include specialists, hospitals, skilled nursing facilities, therapists, and home health-care agencies.

Medicaid:

Public assistance funded through the state to individuals unable to pay for health care. Medicaid can be accessed only when all prior assets and funds are depleted. There are income eligibility criteria that must be met to qualify for Medicaid. Medicaid accounts for about 52% of the nation's care costs and is the source of payment for almost 70% of residents in nursing homes. Medicaid can reimburse nursing facilities for the long-term care of qualifying seniors, and in some states, Medicaid pays for assisted-living care through Medicaid waivers.

Medicare:

A federal health insurance program for people age 65 and older and for individuals with disabilities (from AA). The Social Security Administration administers Medicare regardless of income. It also provides for hospital and nursing facility care (Part A) and physician services, therapies, and home health care (Part B).

Medical Director:

The medical director coordinates with an individual's personal physician to ensure that the facility delivers the care that is prescribed. In some instances, the medical director may be a resident's primary physician. A staff medical director assumes overall responsibility for the formulation and implementation of all policies related to medical care.

Medications Management/Medication Administration:

Formalized procedure with a written set of rules for the management of self-administered medicine, as in an assisted-living setting. A program may include management of the timing and dosage for residents and could include coordination with a resident's personal physician. The resident must take the medication himself or herself. For instance, the facility can remind the resident that she needs to give herself the medicine injection, but the facility cannot perform the actual injection itself.

Non-Ambulatory:

Inability to walk independently; usually bedridden or hospitalized.

Not-for-Profit:

Status of ownership and/or operation characterized by government by community-based boards of trustees who are all volunteers. Board members donate their time and talents to ensure that a not-for-profit organization's approach to caring for older people responds to local needs. Not-for-profit homes and services turn any surplus income back into improving or expanding services for their clients or residents. Many not-for-profit organizations are often associated with religious denominations and fraternal groups. Not-for-profits may also interact with Congress and federal agencies to further causes that serve the elderly.

Nurse Assistant:

Nurse assistants work under the supervision of a registered nurse or licensed practical nurse. A nurse assistant provides the most personal care to residents, including bathing, dressing, and toileting. Must be trained, tested, and certified to provide care in nursing facilities that participate in the Medicare and Medicaid programs.

Nursing Home:

Provides 24-hour skilled care for the more acute patients. Patients generally rely on assistance for most or all daily living activities (such as bathing, dressing, and toileting) (from ALFA). One step below hospital acute care. Regular medical supervision and rehabilitation therapy are mandated to be available, and nursing homes are eligible to participate in the Medicaid program. These facilities are state-licensed. Also referred to as nursing facility or convalescent home. See also Skilled Nursing Facility.

Occupational Therapy:

A creative activity prescribed for its effect in promoting recovery or rehabilitation. This is done to help individuals relearn activities of daily living and is generally administered by a licensed therapist.

Physical Therapy:

The treatment of disease or injury by physical and mechanical means (such as massage, regulated exercise, water, light, heat, and electricity). Physical therapists plan and administer prescribed physical therapy treatment programs for residents to help restore their function and strength.

Quality Care:

Term used to describe care and services that allow recipients to attain and maintain their highest level of mental, physical, and psychological function, in a dignified and caring way.

Registered Nurse (RN):

Graduate trained nurse who has passed a state board examination and is licensed by a state agency to practice nursing. A minimum of 2 years of college is required in addition to passage of the state exams. The RN plans for resident care by assessing resident needs, developing and monitoring care plans in conjunction with physicians, and executing highly technical, skilled nursing treatments.

Rehabilitation:

Therapeutic care for persons requiring intensive physical, occupational, or speech therapy in order to restore the patient to a former capacity.

Respite Care:

Services that provide people with temporary relief from tasks associated with caregiving (e.g., in-home assistance, short nursing home stays, adult day care).

Senior Apartment:

Age-restricted multiunit housing for older adults who are able to care for themselves. Usually no additional services such as meals or transportation are provided. Similar to independent living.

Senior Citizen Policies:

Insurance policies for those over the age of sixty-five. In many cases these policies are in combination with coverage provided by the government under the Medicare program.

Support Group:

Facilitated gathering of caregivers, family, friends, or others affected by a disease or condition for the purpose of discussing issues related to the disease.

Bibliography

Achenbaum, W. A. (1978). *Old age in the new land.* Baltimore, MD: Johns Hopkins University Press.

Allen, J. A., & Burwell, N. Y. (1980). Ageism and racism: Two issues in social work education and practice. *Journal of Education for Social Work, 16*(2), 71–77.

Ansello, E. F. (1977). Age and ageism in children's first literature. *Educational Gerontology, 2*, 255–274.

Arluke, A., & Levin, J. (1984, August-September). Another stereotype: Old age as second childhood. *Aging*, 7–11.

Aronson, B. S. (1966). Personality stereotypes of aging. *Journal of Gerontology, 21*, 458–462.

Austin, D. R. (1985). Attitudes toward old age: A hierarchical study. *The Gerontologist, 25*, 431–434.

Baggett, S., & Dickinson, K. (1978, November). Attitudinal consequences of older adult volunteers in the public school setting. Paper presented at the 31st Annual Scientific Meeting of the Gerontological Society, Dallas.

Barbato, C. A., & Feezel, J. D. (1987). The language of aging in different age groups. *The Gerontologist, 27*, 527–531.

Beere, C. A. (1979). *Women and women's issues: A handbook of tests and measures.* San Francisco: Jossey-Bass.

Beeson, D. (1975). Women in studies of aging: A critique and suggestion. *Social Problems, 23*, 52–59.

Bell, J. (1992). In search of a discourse on aging: The elderly on television. *The Gerontologist, 32*, 305–311.

Bishop, J. M., & Krause, D. R. (1984). Depictions of aging and old age on Saturday morning television. *The Gerontologist, 24*, 91–94.

Block, M. R., Davidson, J. L., & Grambs, J. D. (1981). *Women over forty: Visions and realities.* New York: Springer.

Boone, D. R. (1985). Ageism: A negative view of the aged. *ASHA, 27*, 51–53.

Broverman, I. K., Broverman, D. M., & Rosenkrantz, P. (1972). Sex-role stereotypes: A current appraisal. *Journal of Social Issues, 28*, 59–79.

Brown, J. K. (1985). *In her prime.* Massachusetts: Bergin & Garvey.

Brubaker, T. H., & Powers, E. A. (1976). The stereotype of "old": A review and alternative approach. *Journal of Gerontology, 31*, 441–447.

Busse, I. W. (1968). Viewpoint: Prejudice and gerontology. *The Gerontologist, 8*, 66.

Butler, R. N. (1969). Age-ism: Another form of bigotry. *The Gerontologist, 9*, 243–246.

Butler, R. N. (1975a). Psychiatry and the elderly: An overview. *American Journal of Psychiatry, 132*, 893–900.

Butler, R. N. (1975b). *Why survive? Being old in America.* New York: Harper & Row.

Butler, R. N. (1980). Ageism: A foreword. *Journal of Social Issues, 365*, 8–11.

Butler, R. N., & Lewis, M. I. (1977). *Aging and mental health.* St. Louis: C. V. Mosby.

Cheren, C. E. (Ed.). (1984, August-September). Ageism in America. *Aging*, 346.

Clark, A. N. G., & Anderson, B. (1967). *Culture and aging*. Springfield, IL: Charles C. Thomas.

Cole, T. R. (1992). *The journey of life: A cultural history of aging in America*. Cambridge University Press.

Coe, R. M. (1967). Professional perspectives on the aged. *The Gerontologist, 7*, 114–119.

Comfort, A. (1976). Age prejudice in America. *Social Policy, 7*(3), 3–8.

Crockett, W. H., & Hummert, M. L. (1987). Perceptions of aging and the elderly. In K. W. Schaie (Ed.), *Annual review of gerontology and geriatrics* (Vol. 7, pp. 217–242). New York: Springer.

Datan, N. (1989). Aging women: The silent majority. *Women's Studies Quarterly, 17*, 12–19.

Davies, L. J. (1977). Attitudes toward old age and aging as shown by humor. *The Gerontologist, 17*, 220–226.

Dye, C. J. (1978). Psychologists' role in the provision of mental health care for the elderly. *Professional Psychologist, 9*, 38–49.

Elliott, J. (1984). The daytime television drama portrayal of older adults. *The Gerontologist, 24*, 628–633.

Estes, C. L. (1979). *The aging enterprise*. San Francisco: Jossey-Bass.

Fillmer, H. T. (1982). Sex stereotyping of elderly by children. *Educational Gerontology, 8*, 77–85.

Fischer, D. H. (1978). *Growing old in America*. New York: Oxford University Press.

Goodstein, R. K. (1985). Common clinical problems in the elderly: Camouflaged by ageism and atypical presentation. *Psychiatric Annals, 15,* 299–311.

Green, S. K. (1981). Attitudes and perceptions about the elderly: Current and future Perspectives. *Aging and Human Development, 13,* 95–115.

Greene, R. (1983). Ageism, death anxiety, and the case worker. *Journal of Social Service Research, 7*(1), 55–69.

Gerbner, G., Gross, L., Signorielli, N., & Morgan, M. (1980). Aging with television: Images in television drama and conceptions of social reality. *Journal of Communication, 30,* 37–47.

Golde, P., & Kogan, N. (1958). A sentence completion procedure for assessing attitudes toward old people. *Journal of Gerontology, 14,* 355–363.

Gruman, G. J. (1978). Cultural origins of present-day "ageism": The modernization of the life cycle. In S. F. Spicker, K. M. Woodward, & D. D. Van Tassel (Eds.), *Aging and the elderly: Humanistic perspectives in gerontology* (pp. 359–387).

Gutmann, D. (1985). The cross-cultural perspective: Notes toward a comparative psychology of aging. In R. H. Binstock & E. Shanas (Eds.), *Handbook of aging and the social sciences* (2nd ed.). New York: Van Nostrand Reinhold.

Herrick, J. W. (1983). Interbehavioral perspectives on aging. *International Journal of Aging and Human Development, 16,* 95–124.

Hess, B. B. (1974). Stereotypes of the aged. *Journal of Communication, 24,* 76–85.

Hopkins, T. J. (1980). A conceptual framework for understanding the three "isms": Racism, ageism, sexism. *Journal of Education for Social Work, 16*(2), 63–70.

Hultsch, D. F., & Deutsch, F. (1981). *Adult development and aging: A life-span perspective.* New York: McGraw Hill.

Ivester, C., & King, K. (1977). Attitudes of adolescents toward the aged. *The Gerontologist, 17*, 85–88.

Jantz, F. K., Seefeldt, C., Galper, A., & Serock, K. (1977). Children's attitudes toward the elderly. *Social Education, 41*, 518–523.

Jensen, G. D., & Oakley, F. B. (1982–1983). Ageism across cultures and in perspective of socio-biologic and psychodynamic theories. *International Journal of Aging and Human Development, 15*, 17–26.

Kalish, R. A. (1975). *Late adulthood.* Monterey, CA: Brooks/Cole.

Kastenbaum, R. (1973, April). *On death and dying: Should we have mixed feelings about our ambivalence toward the aged?* Paper presented at an interdisciplinary meeting of the Boston Society of Gerontologic Psychiatry, Boston.

Kastenbaum, R. (1978). Exit existence: Society's unwritten script for old age and death. In D. D. Van Tassel (Ed.), *Aging, death, and the completion of being.* Philadelphia: University of Pennsylvania Press.

Kastenbaum, R., & Durkee, N. (1964a). Elderly people view old age. In R. Kastenbaum (Ed.), *New thoughts on old age.* New York: Springer.

Kastenbaum, R., & Durkee, N. (1964b). Young people view old age. In R. Kastenbaum (Ed.), *New thoughts on old age.* New York: Springer.

Kilty, K. M., & Feld, A. (1976). Attitudes toward aging and toward the needs of older people. *Journal of Gerontology, 31*, 586–594.

Kimmel, D. C. (1988). Ageism, psychology, and public policy. *American Psychologist, 43*, 175–178.

Kite, M. E., & Johnson, B. T. (1988). Attitudes toward older and younger adults: A meta-analysis. *Psychology and Aging, 3*, 232–244.

Kogan, N. (1979). Beliefs, attitudes, and stereotypes about old people: A new look at some old issues. *Research on Aging, 1*, 11–36.

Kravetz, D. F. (1976). Sex-role concepts of women. *Journal of Clinical and Consulting Psychology, 44*, 437–443.

Kuypers, J. A., & Bengtson, V. L. (1973). Social breakdown and competence: A model of normal aging. *Human Development, 16*, 181–201.

Larson, R. (1978). Thirty years of research on the subjective well-being of older Americans. *Journal of Gerontology, 33*, 109–125.

Levenson, A. J. (1981). Ageism: A major deterrent to the introduction of curricula in aging. *Gerontology and Geriatric Education, 1*, 161–162.

Lowenthal, M. F., Thurnher, M., & Chiriboga, D. (1975). *Four stages of life: A comparative study of women and men facing transition.* San Francisco: Jossey-Bass.

Mangen, D. J., & Peterson, W. A. (1982). *Research instruments in social gerontology.* Minneapolis: University of Minnesota Press.

Martel, M. V. (1968). Age-sex roles in American magazine fiction (1830–1955). In B. Neugarten (Ed.), *Middle age and aging.* Chicago: University of Chicago Press.

McTavish, D. G. (1971). Perceptions of old people: A review of research methodologies and findings. *The Gerontologist, 11*, 90–101.

Miller, R. B., & Dodder, R. A. (1980). A revision of Palmore's Facts on Aging Quiz. *The Gerontologist, 20*, 673–679.

Mitchell, J., Wilson, K., Revicki, D., & Parker, L. (1985). Children's perceptions of aging: A multidimensional approach to differences by age, sex, and race. *The Gerontologist, 25*, 182–187.

Northcott, H. C. (1975). Too young, too old - Age in the world of television. *The Gerontologist, 15*, 184–186.

Nuessel, F. H. (1982). The language of ageism. *The Gerontologist, 22,* 273–276.

Palmore, E. (1971). Attitudes toward aging as shown through humor. *The Gerontologist, 11,* 181–186.

Palmore, E. (1977). Facts on aging: A short quiz. *The Gerontologist, 17,* 315–320.

Passuth, P. M., & Cook, F. L. (1985). Effects of television viewing on knowledge and attitudes about older adults: A critical reexamination. *The Gerontologist, 25,* 68–77.

Payne, B. P., & Whittington, F. (1976). Older women - Examination of popular stereotypes and research evidence. *Social Problems, 23,* 488–504.

Peacock, E. W., & Talley, W. M. (1984). Intergenerational contact: A way to counteract ageism. *Educational Gerontology, 10,* 13–24.

Peterson, D. A. (1985). Toward a definition of educational gerontology. In R. H. Sherron & D. B. Lumsden (Eds.), *Introduction to educational gerontology* (2nd ed., pp. 1–29). Washington, DC: Hemisphere.

Petersen, M. (1973). The visibility and image of old people on television. *Journalism Quarterly, 50,* 568–573.

Ramsdell, M. L. (1973). The trauma of TV's troubled soap families. *Family Coordinator, 22,* 299–304.

Ray, D. C., McKinney, K. A., & Ford, C. V. (1987). Differences in psychologist's ratings of older and younger clients. *The Gerontologist, 27,* 82–86.

Richman, J. (1977). The foolishness and wisdom of age: Attitudes toward the elderly as reflected in jokes. *The Gerontologist, 17,* 210–219.

Riley, M., & Foner, A. (1968). *Aging and society, Vol. I. An inventory of research findings.* New York: Russell Sage Foundation.

Rodin, J., & Langer, E. J. (1980). Aging labels: The decline of control and the fall of self-esteem. *Journal of Social Issues, 36,* 12–29.

Rosencranz, H. A., & McNevin, T. E. (1968). A factor analysis of attitudes toward the aged. *The Gerontologist, 8,* 55–58.

Rosenkrantz, P., Vogel, S., Bee, H., Broverman, I., & Broverman, D. M. (1968). Sex-role stereotypes and self-concepts in college students. *Journal of Clinical and Consulting Psychology, 32,* 287–285.

Ross, M., Tait, R., Brandeberry, L., Grossberg, G., & Nakra, R. (1986). *Age differences in emotional and physical health.* Poster presentation, Midwest Psychological Association, Chicago.

Schaie, K. W. (1988). Ageism in psychological research. *American Psychologist, 43,* 179–183.

Schmidt, D. F., & Boland, S. M. (1986). Structure of perceptions of older adults: Evidence for multiple stereotypes. *Psychology and Aging, 1,* 255–260.

Schonfield, D. (1982). Who is stereotyping whom and why? *The Gerontologist, 22,* 267–272.

Silverman, M. (1977). The old man as women: Detecting stereotypes of aged men with a femininity scale. *Perceptual and Motor Skills, 44,* 336–338.

Slater, P. E. (1964). Cross-cultural views of the aged. In R. Kastenbaum (Ed.), *New thoughts on old age.* New York: Springer.

Swenson, C. F. (1983). A respectable old age. *American Psychologist, 38,* 327–333.

Thomas, E. C., & Yamamoto, K. (1975). Attitudes toward age: An exploration in school-age children. *International Journal of Aging and Human Development, 6,* 117–129.

Tibbits, C. (1979). Can we invalidate negative stereotypes in aging? *The Gerontologist, 19,* 10–20.

Traxler, A. J. (1980). *Let's get gerontologized: Developing a sensitivity to aging. The multi-purpose senior center concept: A training manual for practitioners working with the aging.* Springfield, IL: Illinois Department of Aging.

Tuckman, J., & Lavell, M. (1957). Self-classification as old or not old. *Geriatrics, 12,* 666–671.

Tuckman, J., & Lorge, I. (1953). Attitudes toward old people. *Journal of Social Psychology, 37,* 249–260.

U.S. Bureau of Census (1983). *America in transition: An aging society.* Current Population Reports, Series P-23, No. 128. Washington, DC: Government Printing House.

Weinberger, L. E. (1979). Stereotyping of the elderly: Elementary school children's responses. *Research of Aging, 1,* 113–136.

Weinberger, L. E., & Millham, J. (1975). A multi-dimensional, multiple method analysis of attitudes toward the elderly. *Journal of Gerontology, 30,* 343–348.

Wilensky, H., & Barmack, J. (1966). Interests of doctoral students in clinical psychology in work with older people. *Journal of Gerontology, 21,* 410–414.

Wilson, J. F., & Hafferty, F. W. (1983). Long-term effects of a seminar on aging and health for first-year medical students. *The Gerontologist, 23,* 319–324.

Wilhite, M. J., & Johnson, D. M. (1976). Changes in nursing students' stereotypic attitudes toward old people. *Nursing Research, 25,* 430–432.

Zinberg, N. E. (1976). Normal psychology of the aging process, revisited (I): Social learning and self-image in aging. *Journal of Geriatric Psychiatry, 9,* 131–150.

Bibliography
Homelessness among Older Adults

Abdul-Hamid, W. (1997). The elderly homeless men in Bloomsbury hostels: Their needs for services. *International Journal of Geriatric Psychiatry, 12,* 724–727.

Berman, R., Iris, M., & Keigher, S. (1991). Rethinking homelessness: The homeless and near-homeless elderly in Chicago. *Housing and Society, 18*(2), 13–25.

Bissonnette, A., & Hijjazi, K. (1994). Elder homelessness: A community perspective. *Nursing Clinics of North America, 29,* 409–416.

Cohen, C. (1999). Aging and homelessness. *The Gerontologist, 39,* 5–14.

Cohen, C., & Sokolovsky, J. (1983). Toward a concept of homelessness among aged men. *Journal of Gerontology, 38*(1), 81–89.

Damrosch, S., & Strasser, J. (1988). The homeless elderly in America. *Journal of Gerontological Nursing, 14*(10), 26–29.

DeMallie, D., North, C., & Smith, E. (1997). Psychiatric disorders among the homeless: A comparison of older and younger groups. *The Gerontologist, 37*(1), 61–66.

Doolin, J. (1986). Planning for the special needs of the homeless elderly. *The Gerontologist, 26,* 229–231.

Hudson, B., Rauch, B., Dawson, G., Santos, J., & Burdick, D. (1990). Homelessness: Special problems related to training, research, and the elderly. *Gerontology and Geriatrics Education, 10*(3), 31–69.

Reilly, F. (1994). An ecological approach to health risk: A case study of urban elderly homeless people. *Public Health Nursing, 11*(5), 305–314.

Sullivan, M. (1991). The homeless older woman in context: Alienation, cutoff and re-connection. *Journal of Women and Aging, 3*(2), 3–24.

978-0-595-36476-3
0-595-36476-4